MONET'S
CATHEDRAL
ROUEN 1892 – 1894

KNOPF
75
YEARS·OF·PUBLISHING

MONET'S
CATHEDRAL

ROUEN 1892 – 1894

—

JOACHIM PISSARRO

ALFRED A. KNOPF
NEW YORK
1990

THIS IS A BORZOI BOOK
PUBLISHED BY ALFRED A. KNOPF, INC.

Text copyright © Joachim Pissarro 1990.
Design and typesetting copyright © Breslich & Foss 1990.

All rights reserved under International and Pan-American Copyright Conventions.
Published in the United States by Alfred A. Knopf, Inc., New York. Distributed by
Random House, Inc., New York.

Library of Congress Cataloging-in-Publication Data

Pissarro, Joachim.
    Monet's cathedral: Rouen. 1892-94/Joachim Pissarro.
      p. cm.
    ISBN 0-394-58871-1: $35.00
      1. Monet, Claude, 1840-1926 — Criticism and interpretation.
    2. Cathédrale Notre-Dame (Rouen, France) in art.   I. Title.
    ND553.M7P58   1990
    759.4 — dc20   90-53074
                                                                                CIP

Originally published in Great Britain by Pavilion Books, London.

Manufactured in Spain.
FIRST AMERICAN EDITION

Conceived and produced by Breslich & Foss, Golden House,
28–31 Great Pulteney Street, London W1R 3DD

Designed by Nigel Partridge
Edited by Judy Martin

CONTENTS

INTRODUCTION

On 10 May 1895, the Durand-Ruel galleries in Paris opened their doors to the public for an unusual exhibition of paintings by Claude Monet. Of the fifty paintings exhibited, twenty depicted a single subject – the cathedral of Rouen.

Besides these twenty exhibited views, there were ten more canvases in the same series that remained in Monet's studio at Giverny. Altogether, thirty paintings had been executed by the artist over two separate periods of work in Rouen. They showed the cathedral under different lights, weather conditions and seasonal effects. Monet had begun painting a first group of canvases at the beginning of February in 1892. With some interruptions, due both to family circumstances and professional commitments, Monet's work in Rouen in 1892 lasted until mid-April. In mid-February of 1893, Monet set off on a second campaign, grappling once again with the difficult task of painting Rouen Cathedral. Once again, he returned to Giverny in mid-April of the same year, by which time he had achieved the total of thirty canvases that constitute the *Cathedral* series.

Back at the studio in Giverny, almost all of the cathedral paintings were reworked by the artist from memory, far away from the actual subject. They were thus given a unity and cohesion as a whole group of works that makes it impossible to distinguish on purely stylistic grounds between the first group of views begun in 1892 and the second group painted in Rouen in 1893. It is, however, possible to distinguish the two groups chronologically by analysing the artist's vantage point in front of the cathedral, which shifted slightly from 1892 to 1893.

It was during Monet's reworkings at Giverny that each of the thirty paintings lost its prime originality as a statement of the artist's immediate impression jotted down on canvas in front of the cathedral. Once Monet had reworked and elaborated them together in order to form a coherent ensemble, a series (or 'suite', in the critical vocabulary of the nineteenth century), the paintings were signed and dated 1894, all but three which remained undated. Two paintings seem not to have been reworked.

Monet indicated, as was clearly emphasized in his correspondence, that the cathedrals were not visible to the public, were not available to dealers or collectors, and were not to leave his studio, until they had undergone the whole complex and painstaking process of 'finition'. Monet stressed the point to his dealer, Paul Durand-Ruel, in a letter written from Rouen dated 22 March 1892: "From now on, I refuse to sell my canvases in advance, I want to finish them first, and without rushing, and in the course of time I will choose which ones I will sell."

This raises the question of what Monet meant by 'finish'. It seems particularly relevant to ask the question in the case of the cathedrals, as we have to wonder not only how to approach each individual work as a finished canvas but, furthermore, what the totality of the completed series implies.

On 8 March 1892, in a slightly mellower tone, Monet had written a letter to his wife-to-be, Alice Hoschedé, mentioning a request he had received from the private collector Depeaux to acquire two of the cathedral paintings. "As I could have guessed [Depeaux] asked to be put at the top of the list for a cathedral – one for himself and one for the Musée de Rouen. But even though I took note of his request, I could not part with any of my canvases before being through with the whole thing, and before seeing them and seeing them again back in Giverny."

It is in a famous letter to Gustave Geffroy, sent from Rouen on 28 March 1893, that one senses most clearly the difficulty that the problem of 'finishing' the *Cathedral* series could present for Monet: "My stay here is coming to a close; this does not mean, however, that I am anywhere near to finishing my cathedrals. Alas! I can only repeat the same thing: that is that the more I advance, the tougher it becomes for me to render what I feel; and I am thinking inside that anybody who says that he has finished a canvas is frightfully arrogant. Finishing means complete, perfect, I am working relentlessly without progressing."

We are faced here with a problem of definition regarding, specifically, the series of the *Cathedrals*, to which these three letters refer. In the last letter, in particular, Monet defines a finished work as "complete" and "perfect". On the other hand, in the same letter Monet implicitly rules out the possibility of ever finishing any work: the claim to have "finished" a work of art is, according to Monet, an unreasonable pretension. Monet's position parallels the mathematical concept of an asymptotical curve, progressing infinitely toward a goal while never quite reaching it.

While this book purports to offer a complete view of the whole series of Monet's paintings of Rouen Cathedral, Monet's letters written while he was working on these paintings point to the problem raised by the very notion of a complete series. Monet's choice of the cathedral of Rouen as subject matter for his series constitutes a major break in the painter's career and, arguably, a turning point in the history of modern painting. The series deals expressly, and in a climactic sense, with the notion of the impossibility of finishing a painting.

At first glance, the series of the *Cathedrals* is based on a twofold paradox. Each of the thirty views of the cathedral, while striving to render a pictorial account of the artist's fleeting, momentary sensation of the cathedral under some ephemeral light effect, was the result of months and months of work. Further, although each different view of the cathedral represents a separate moment, an individual and separate slice of time and light as perceived by the artist in front of the cathedral, everything in Monet's working process and in his letters indicates that the paintings were conceived, thought out and worked out together, and as such were almost inseparable. Not only is each painting as a unit almost unfinishable, but the whole cycle of the series as a unified representation of time is in essence limitless. Yet all of these works are bound together by the same intense pictorial experimentation: each of the thirty paintings of the cathedral can be looked at and apprehended as an individual unit of an exploratory sequence, but all individually gain sense when they are replaced within the context of the whole series.

To this extent, the *Cathedral* series can be seen as exactly refuting the definition of Impressionism suggested by a contemporary critic of the Impressionists, who saw in it "the rapid noting of illusive appearance".[1] This account was published in 1893, the year the cathedral paintings were being 'finished'. The author, George Moore, who was well acquainted with the Impressionists, might not have known of Monet's work in progress. Applying his definition to Monet's *Cathedrals*, one could reasonably describe the effect of a ray of sunshine on the façade of a cathedral as an "illusive appearance"; yet the execution of thirty meticulously worked out canvases over a span of two years was anything but "the rapid noting of an illusive appearance."

In a remarkable recent article, R.R. Bernier has argued that Monet in the 1870s founded a "new mode of representation" that was read by the critics of the time as the result of an "inadequate perception of nature" or more simply as a "distortion of nature". Monet's sketchiness in his paintings, the lack of resolution in his work, seemed to fail "to present convincingly the visual experience."[2] Consequently, his work could be sneered at as amounting to a mere "smattering, rubbing, smearing, hurling, flinging, jabbing."[3]

Bernier reads the first developments of Monet's work as the battle of "the preliminary sketch versus the finished picture" by opposing "the infinite extendability of our perception" to the traditional devices "that had always constituted the very basis of illusionism in painting: convincing spatial relations between objects marked by changes in scale, overlap of one form by another, relative degrees of clarity and focus, smooth scale of tonal variation in colour and gradation in modelling – by which, it was felt, the world was given density and credibility."[4]

In theory, the *Cathedral* series that is presented completely in this book is incompletable. Monet's series of the cathedral categorically does away with the traditional notion of a 'finished work of art', an essential precept of contemporary Salon art. As Monet in his mid-fifties was starting to enjoy greater financial success and wider repute, he felt he could clearly express his annoyance at the "frightful arrogance" of those Salon painters or their like who claimed superiority for the perfection and polish that a fully completed Salon painting presented.

But the singularity and unique force of the *Cathedral* series resides elsewhere. Whereas R.R. Bernier sees a correspondence between Monet's new mode of representation and "an almost unseizable subject matter", the *Cathedral* series, unlike Monet's previous series paintings, constitutes a serious limitation to this correspondence. Bernier examines a continuum between Monet's "very 'incomplete' procedure" and his fleeting subject matters: between "paint-marks and moving figures" or "between broad sweeps of colour and the ambiguous configurations in nature".[5] This analysis adequately applies to such works as *La Grenouillère*, *Le Boulevard des Capucines*, or *Le Soleil couchant sur la Seine, effet d'hiver*.

However, none of these "ambiguous configurations" can be found in the strictly defined, well delineated architectural and ornamented structure of the Gothic façade. Rouen Cathedral stands as a monolith whose rigidity, permanence and massive unity is impermeable. In fact, a direct contradiction can be found between Monet's procedure – which we have seen is essentially incompletable – and his subject matter – the firmly rooted, unchanging immobility of a Gothic stone façade, as seen and traditionally revealed by the extensive iconography of Rouen Cathedral. As opposed to the poplars, the subject of a previous series, whose trembling leaves screen the freckling light and impress the viewer with an effect of constant mobility, or to the haystacks built out of lightweight material and easily disposable from year to year, the cathedral – static, permanent, massive – does not seem to offer the most fecund material for the rendering of an artist's fleeting sensations.

In a major sense, Monet's *Cathedral* series constituted a considerable challenge – not only a climactic challenge to Salon art and the notion of finished art, but also a challenge to Monet himself, through the selection of a subject most resistant to his observation of the changes of light, weather and atmosphere. It creates, equally, a challenge to the senses of the viewer, by putting the greatest demand on the flexibility of our perception.

We can thus understand why Monet, referring to all of the cathedral paintings, felt it was so important that he should "see them and see them again in my studio". Georges Clemenceau immediately understood the necessity of seeing the cathedrals altogether. In his review of the 1895 exhibition, he wrote: "How come there has not been a millionaire to understand, even dimly, the meaning of these twenty cathedrals put altogether and to say: 'I buy the lot', as he would have done with a bundle of shares."

Among Monet's colleagues, Camille Pissarro sensed acutely that these paintings should be seen together. In a letter to his son, dated 26 May 1895, he wrote: "His cathedrals are going to be scattered here and there, and yet it is as a whole that it must be seen." And later, on 1 June 1895: "I so much wish that you could have seen this as a whole, for I find in this a superb unity that I have been seeking for so long. I find the whole thing so important that I came only to see it."

THE ORIGINS OF THE CATHEDRAL SERIES

It is practically impossible to form a complete understanding of Monet's pictorial progression towards the formation of the *Cathedral* series without looking at the fascinating pictorial dialogue between Pissarro and Monet around the mythical essence of Rouen and its poetical evocation through Impressionism. As Christopher Lloyd has pointed out, Pissarro clearly underlined this aspect of Rouen as a source of pictorial imagery by comparing it to Venice, that most vital stimulus to artistic imagination. During his own most successful artistic venture in Rouen, in 1896, Pissarro wrote to his son Lucien: "It is as beautiful as Venice … it has wonderful character and truly it is beautiful."

Lloyd explains Pissarro's fascination with the city of Rouen: "for Pissarro, Rouen possessed a potency that Venice had once exerted, and indeed continues to exert, on the European consciousness. In both cities there was a similar magic in the effects derived from the aesthetic relationship between the buildings and the water – in Rouen the Seine, and in Venice the lagoon or the canals."[1] Monet and Pissarro both responded in their ways to the magic of Rouen, reactivating and transforming a visual interest that had been notably explored by Claude Lorrain and J.M.W. Turner. Monet's *Cathedral* series crucially engages with the artistic fascination exerted by Rouen on the contemporary imagination.

Monet was familiar with Rouen from childhood. Although he was born in Paris, in 1840, to Parisian parents, in 1845 the family moved to Le Havre when Monet's father joined the fairly prosperous trade business of his sister and brother-in-law, the Lecadres. On the train journey from Paris to Le Havre, Monet would have discovered for the first time the Gothic city of Rouen, on the river Seine almost halfway between the capital city and the coastal port. Later in life, Monet's older brother Léon established himself as a chemist in Rouen and made his home in the nearby village of

Vue de Rouen 1872, Claude Monet, Private Collection

Déville. This family connection offered Claude Monet several occasions to visit the city, but it was some time before he chose to look upon it with a painter's eye and to make use of aspects of Rouen as subject matter for his paintings.

Monet's first paintings of Rouen and its surroundings date back to 1872, exactly two decades before the *Cathedral* series was initiated. Little attention is usually paid to this group of thirteen paintings, done in the middle of the prolific and inspired Argenteuil period. Monet had been living and working at Argenteuil for over a year, painting brilliant river scenes shimmering with silvery patches of light, heightened by the vivid hues of the sky and the sailboats reflected on the water. In 1872 he interrupted this period of intense productivity to participate in a municipal exhibition in Rouen, doubtless at the invitation of his brother Léon.

The waters of the Seine flow through both towns, passing from Argenteuil about 100 kilometres downstream to Rouen. The groups of paintings executed in Argenteuil and Rouen carry out essentially the same pictorial concerns and the same compositional themes and devices. The Rouen pictures include a couple of industrial views and, predominantly, landscapes seen at a distance with, in the foreground, sailboats and rowing boats of varied scale. In three of these thirteen paintings, the cathedral of Rouen is depicted.

In particular, in *View of Rouen*, the cathedral appears in a prominent and imposing position. This is in fact one of the most remarkable paintings from the Rouen period of 1872. The composition was conceived overall with ample control and great pictorial intelligence. Horizontally, the painting is organized in a formal tension between three elements: water (the Seine river that offers the painter his vantage point, as this painting seems most likely to have been executed from a boat) occupying about one-third of the picture surface; the sky, with its clouds reflecting in the Seine, occupying over half the picture surface; and the earth, a horizontal stretch of land squeezed between sky and water, where the city of Rouen stands with the Côte Sainte Catherine on the right and the two islands of Brouilly and Lacroix on the left.

The picture presents a series of counterbalancing groups of verticals that establish a solid and active rhythm throughout the canvas. From left to right, the viewer's eye travels across a series of dark, thin lines depicting the scant tree trunks on the two islands, then encounters the two tall verticals of boats' masts that bring together the top and bottom of the composition, the sky and the river. These two verticals echo the tower and the spire of the cathedral in rigorously symmetrical order. The four vertical axes (the two boat poles, the tower and the spire) form a compositional reversal that can be read indifferently from left to right or from right

to left: tall, small; small, tall. Lastly, at the right-hand side a mass of trees and houses stands erect, corresponding to the group of trees on the extreme left.

This extraordinary organization of compositional devices would offer little "sense" to the viewer if it did not purport to heighten the special importance of one element – the cathedral. Seen from the distance, the cathedral stands downstream with its tower and spire hovering over the thin stretch of land where small houses surround its base. It is placed almost at the centre of the composition. The reflection of the cathedral stretches across the surface of the river towards the foreground of the painting, creating a dominant vertical emphasis, just off-centre, that unifies the three basic horizontal elements of the composition – water, sky, earth.

In this painting, one of Monet's very first views of Rouen, the cathedral is seen as the core of the composition, offering a portent of the significance of the cathedral and the role that it would play in Monet's painting twenty years later. It also provides a strong foretaste of Monet's predominant pictorial concern with unifying the elementary diversity into a harmonious whole, a function which the *Cathedral* series subsequently carried out to its extreme.

Gustave Geffroy, Monet's first biographer, had earlier emphasized this particularly important factor of unification in Monet's work. About Monet's paintings of Belle-Ile in Brittany of 1886, Geffroy wrote: "Monet, painter of the sea, is at the same time a painter of the air and sky."[2] "His paintings are seen as a whole. All these shapes, all these shimmers order each other, saturate each other, influence each other with their mutual colours and reflections (…) Hence, the unity of his paintings which reveal the shape of the seashore and at the same time the movement of the sea, they indicate the time of day through the colour of the rocks and the colour of the sea."

It seems that this systematic impulse, at work to various degrees throughout Monet's pictorial career, was an essential constitutive force in the series of paintings of the cathedral.

View of Rouen was painted two decades before the series of Rouen Cathedral, and Monet could easily have forgotten it in the meantime. However, when in 1883 Durand-Ruel organized one-man shows dedicated to each of the Impressionists, and Monet's paintings formed the first exhibition, artist and dealer selected the 1872 view of Rouen to feature in this essential showcase of Monet's work.[3] Furthermore, an important review of the exhibition by Alfred de Lostalot appeared in the *Gazette des Beaux-Arts*.[4] Monet made a few drawings to illustrate this article and one of these drawings was executed after his painting, *View of Rouen*. This drawing establishes a continuity of interest on Monet's part that links the 1872 paintings at Rouen, which had included his initial pictorial response to the

Vue de Rouen 1883, Claude Monet, Sterling & Francine Clark Art Institute, Williamstown, MASS

cathedral, to the later series focusing on the cathedral alone.

Although Monet castigated his first one-man show as a *"four"* (a flop)[5] Pissarro, who naturally visited this important event, hailed it as *"merveilleuse"*.[6] In all likelihood, Pissarro would have also read de Lostalot's article and noticed Monet's drawing. It is interesting to think that these images of Rouen by Monet may have had some impact on Pissarro's decision to go to Rouen a few months later, in October 1883, to renew his own range of subject matter.

This hypothesis is strengthened by the fact that, in the year following the Monet retrospective at Durand-Ruel, Pissarro produced an etching depicting Rouen Cathedral quite reminiscent compositionally of Monet's *View of Rouen* of 1872 and the 1883 drawing after the painting. Pissarro's print seems to focus on Rouen Cathedral from a similar viewpoint to that of Monet's painting, although it has notably different characteristics. The vantage point is the bank of the river; Pissarro is standing on the earth while sketching his subject, whereas Monet had worked from a boat on the river in 1872. In the etching the cathedral, standing erect and massive, with its deep, plunging reflection on the water's surface, occupies over three-quarters of the height of the image. Furthermore, the reflection in the Seine is far more substantial and present than in Monet's drawing of the cathedral. The image contributes to a progressive centralization of the cathedral motif that came to its most extreme representation in Monet's series paintings. One could almost write the history of Monet's *Cathedral* series as one would follow the various steps of a zoom-lens closing in on a given subject, and in this sense the viewpoint of Pissarro's print constitutes a distinctive step towards a closer and yet less detailed approach to the monument.

There is some significance to the fact that this etching, *View of Rouen (Cours la Reine)*, was held by the artist to be sufficiently important to be included in the eighth and last Impressionist exhibition of 1886, in which Pissarro included seven prints together with his paintings. Among the seven prints, four depicted Rouen subjects. Pissarro chose to give prominence to the prints of Rouen in an exhibition where he was to be confronted by the latest work of all of his colleagues. Also, since Monet must have seen the etching in the exhibition, a further connection is established between the two artists' responses to Rouen over a continuing period.

Monet's drawing was a virtual copy of his 1872 painting intended specifically to be reproduced in print accompanying de Lostalot's article. The two graphic works, Monet's drawing and Pissarro's print, resorting to linear structures and black and white tonal values, are most interesting for notable differences from each other and from the *Cathedral* series of 1892. It is rather curious that two of the earliest Impressionist precedents for the series were both meant to be reproduced, or printed. However, the chasm between the two methods is vast. Monet's drawing was printed typographically in the *Gazette des Beaux-Arts* and reproduced identically in each issue of the art periodical. Pissarro's etching was printed on a hand-operated press, and went through three different states. Of the first state, one proof is known. There are four existing proofs of the second state, numbered two to five, and about ten proofs of the third state.

In his work at Rouen, Pissarro developed the first premise of an interest in series *per se*.[7] He furthered this novel interest in serial procedures by exploiting the technical devices offered by printing as a medium. He experimented with the etched image in different ways: each state of the print offered a different work, a different treatment of the motif. In the first state, for instance, the sky lacks detail as compared to the subsequent states, and elaboration of the hills and trees later worked in drypoint is not yet visible. The second state shows the sky overloaded with fresh work. The third state appears as a sort of synthesis of the previous two, as some of the work done in the second state has been erased, particularly in the sky and water.

Vue de Rouen (Cours-La-Reine) 1883, *Camille Pissarro, British Museum, London*

Not only was each separate state necessarily different and unique, but in accordance with the nature of the etching process, each proof of each state had individual characteristics. According to how much ink the artist would apply to the plate, according to how he would modulate the nuances between the etched areas and the flat areas, how much whitening he would use, how strongly the pressure of the press was set, each impression (proof) would necessarily vary.

This is another essential difference between Monet's drawing of his *View of Rouen* and Pissarro's print. Because of the method by which Monet's drawing was reproduced, each illustration was absolutely identical to the next. Pissarro, incidentally, on a few occasions voiced his horror for the process of mechanical reproduction, called *gillotage*, for which Monet's drawing had been conceived. Comparing this process to "real print", Pissarro once wrote: "Gillotage is to engraving what fake Turkish rugs are to the real ones." In the same letter, commenting on the results obtained by *Le Figaro* through this printing process, he wrote: "They didn't have to go so far to do so badly, it's horrible, horrible!!"[8]

In a sense, the drawings made for publication were closer in their function, although not in execution, to photography. As soon as Durand-Ruel started to use photography as a means of reproduction, these drawings lost their *raison d'être*. As John House explained: "The drawings that Monet executed for publication were meant to translate in black and white the effect of complete oil painting. They suggest complex effects of lighting and textures and evoke the gestures of the brush by vigorous graphic strokes of charcoal or crayon, designed to echo, in rough and in miniature, the copied painting; free linear contours play some part in them, but their effect is achieved by the massing of gradated tonal values, standing for the coloured nuances of the painting. Though they often succeed well in this aim, they have no independent status in Monet's creative process, and were simply the results of the demands of their prospective publishers."[9]

In the 1883 drawing, Monet's view of the cathedral from the 1872 painting underwent a process of impoverishment. It is interesting to note that besides all the reductive process inherent in the translation of a painting into a drawing (as described by House), Monet's drawing of the cathedral is much more detailed, conventional and careful than its 1872 painted model. The reflection of the cathedral on the water surface, which was momentous in the 1872 painting, has dissolved into a pale and rarified shadow in the 1883 drawing. The buildings below the cathedral that were not originally given much status are in the drawing minutely detailed – the number of windows can almost be counted on each building.

If Monet, in his drawings, reverted to a more traditional,

iconographically recognizable, analytical style, Camille Pissarro's print offered quite the reverse. There we can see the mass of the cathedral placed centrally in the three different states of the etching, each offering a different treatment of the overall *enveloppe* that surrounds the cathedral. The image of the cathedral in the print takes a strong stance against a primarily linear treatment of the subject as seen in Monet's drawing. Pissarro does not intend to distinguish between the various compositional elements, hence he creates a sense of overall unity in the work; even the two characters walking on the bank seem to fit into the same mould that cast the entire print.

Describing the printing technique of Pissarro in those years, Michel Melot wrote: "Pissarro blends together a whole background formed with very distinct elements in reality that a classical painter would first have separated one from the other ..."[10] Then, describing the *Haystacks* by Pissarro, Melot underscores a graphic device which is very much at work in the etched view of Rouen: "It's the shadow cast by the haystacks under the setting sun that cannot be distinguished from the object that casts it. In this way the impressionist draughtsman lays as principle that the shadow and the reality are one and the same in their representation, it goes the same way with reflection and reality – potential object and real object."[11]

Pissarro confers the same density on the reflection of the cathedral in the Seine river as on the cathedral itself, and he renders with equal weight the sky, the air and the water. This device, which Pissarro obtained through his so-called *manière grise* (grey manner), resulted from rubbing some sandpaper on the zinc plate, in the sky and on the water surface, in order to suggest a certain movement and animate the entire surface of the work. At the same time, this reduced the impact of the linear definition of the various elements in the composition and gave the whole print much more homogeneity. Pissarro's print, far more so than Monet's drawing, appears in keeping with Monet's intention, as recorded by Theodore Robinson: "I have searched for the same thing as always; I have wanted to do architecture without doing its features, without the lines."[12]

It is interesting and rather curious that Pissarro's etching *View of Rouen*, rarely reproduced and almost never quoted, has so far escaped the abundant and sustained efforts towards critical interpretation of Monet's *Cathedral* series. Camille Pissarro's print, in three states and various proofs (or impressions) lays the procedural and technical ground for Monet's series of 1892–93. Pissarro's print, like Monet's series paintings and unlike Monet's drawing of 1883, does not aim at identifying the building it depicts. Rather, the print, through its states, develops impressions left on the artist's retina by the motif.

There is a special relevance in this discussion to the two meanings of the word "impression". On the one hand, it means the effect of an encompassing and immediate perception of things, but it is also used in the specific context of printing to signify the transfer of an engraved motif from a plate to a sheet of paper.

Pissarro and Degas had introduced a major break in the traditional concept of print, insofar as they had ceased totally to consider each state of a print as a technical "step" toward the fabrication of a desirable finished and perfect "end result" – the final state. In 1880, Pissarro had for the first time exhibited different states of the same print together, in the Fourth Impressionist Exhibition. Pissarro and Degas had introduced the habit of numbering and signing each state, and also each proof (impression) of each state. As Melot explained, "when they are put together, the various states of a print give it an altogether different meaning. The work of art is composed out of all its states. They cannot be considered separately. They form a series, which does not even imply any direction nor any end, of different impressions of the same motif (...) They do not tend toward a final result, but they are as many equivalent versions of the same vision – an inacceptable conception to the mind of the Academy student in search of an absolute ideal."[13]

Clearly, we are standing here within close reach of Monet's *Cathedral* series, realized ten years later. Both Pissarro's print and Monet's series of paintings of the cathedral do away with the idea of a permanent reality, preexistent to the vision of an artist. It is a noteworthy coincidence that one of the principal implications of these works was to refute the notion of a solid, objective vision of an immobile and permanent reality, while at the same time scientific investigation was moving toward similar conclusions. For example, in 1889 it was proved mathematically, in a very detailed study by Henri Poincaré, that not a single place, no "referential", could be held as totally immobile since, as Herschl had observed in the eighteenth century, an object that is immobile on the surface of the earth is not, if one considers its position in relation to the sun; and likewise it cannot be held immobile in relation to the earth, since the whole solar system is in movement. This crucial statement might sound obvious to the modern reader, but in the context of the late nineteenth century Poincaré's demonstration had very far-reaching consequences.

In their graphic and pictorial experiments, Monet and Pissarro were dealing with the same themes and notions that were at the root of some fundamental scientific discoveries occurring contemporaneously. Although this cannot be the subject of an in-depth study within these pages, it is extraordinary to realize that as these artists were, in their individual ways, transforming the usual notion of one's perception of reality through their experiments with "series", relativizing everything, scientists were conducting parallel investigations into the relationships of energy and matter in the physical world. This seems to illustrate the idea that certain themes have a common destiny. The traditionally incompatible notions of mass, light and energy found their pictorial resolution in the visual and poetical blending of Monet's *Cathedral* series of 1892–93, as they found a scientific and theoretical resolution in Einstein's notes in the *Annalen der Physik* of 1905.

What is interesting about the particular motif in Monet's 1872 painting, his 1883 drawing, and Pissarro's etching, is that it is iconographically an impressionistic motif of the cathedral, as opposed to the *Cathedral* series itself, for instance, which is more post-impressionistic in approach. After 1883, there is no trace of this view as painted from a boat (Monet, 1872) or sketched from the river bank (Pissarro, 1883). This is the only group of works known to us in which the reflection of the cathedral on the surface of the river plays a significant role in the organization of the composition.

There is one other painting requiring mention here that actually includes the river Seine as a conspicuous compositional element. This is the 1883 painting by Camille Pissarro entitled *La Cathédrale de Rouen*. In this image the cathedral still stands in the background, although the artist here seems closer to his subject than in the works previously examined. Everything seems to be at a right angle to something else – roofs-spire, trees-ramp, sailboat-river. This is a seemingly simple picture with a forthright, plain, frontal visual effect, but it has two particularly distinctive features with regard to the progression towards the *Cathedral* series.

The first is that the central neo-Gothic spire, taller than either of the two western towers of the cathedral, actually hides the Tour Saint Romain. We attend here a selection process which is the exact opposite of what Monet decided to do in the *Cathedral* series: in the series, the spire is hidden by the towers. In fact, Pissarro is looking at the cathedral from the south-east, whereas Monet concentrated on the western façade. The tower that can be seen on the left in Pissarro's painting is the Tour de Beurre, the tower that partly appears on the right in some of Monet's *Cathedrals*.

The second feature is that this is the last painting in which the element of water plays an important role in the impressionist

La Cathédrale de Rouen 1883, *Camille Pissarro, Document Archives Durand-Ruel, Paris*

pictorial treatment of the cathedral. In no work after 1883 is the view from or across the water to be found, as in Monet's 1872 painting and Pissarro's print. The reflection of the cathedral as a pictorial theme has been exhausted. Monet and Pissarro moved on to other concerns. The overall, much more complex *enveloppe*, the atmospheric elements surrounding the cathedral, became of increasing interest to Monet, while the constant flow of human traffic piqued Pissarro's curiosity – he was led to deal with movement, mess, chaos. When Pissarro later resumed his interest in the cathedral, it was to plot it in the middle of the ceaseless human traffic in a vegetable market – something completely unthinkable in Monet's terms.

In 1892, just before focusing on the west portal of the cathedral, Monet produced three paintings, two of which were panoramic views of the town seen from uphill, while the third painting was a view of the Rue de l'Epicerie, leading to the south entrance of the cathedral. Both motifs have a history in the context of the Impressionist iconography of Rouen.

The first motif seems to have always captured the pictorial imagination of the Impressionists. Rouen, seen from far above, from the Côte Bonsecours, sits in the middle of its valley with its many spires piercing through the undefined layers of vapours. This motif is itself rooted in the literary imagination of the nineteenth century, which Gustave Flaubert exploited to a fascinating degree. In *Madame Bovary*, Flaubert resorts to a visual description of the heroine's village, Yonville, which, although written forty years before Monet's panoramic views of Rouen were painted, could almost be read as a literary transcription of Monet's imagery.

"It was in the first days of October. There was fog over the countryside. The vapours were spreading themselves across the horizon, against the contours of the hills; and others, tearing themselves apart, were rising and becoming lost. Sometimes, in a stretched gap between the clouds, under a ray of sun, the roofs of Yonville could be seen in the distance, with the gardens on the water's edge, the courtyards, the walls, and the church steeple. Emma half-closed her eyes to make out her house, and never had this poor village where she lived appeared so small to her. From the height at which they were, the whole valley appeared to be an immense pale lake, evaporating into the air."

In another passage from the same novel, direct reference is made to the fogs of Rouen seen from afar through Emma Bovary's eyes. Emma, in the arms of her lover, catches a glimpse of Rouen in the distance surrounded by its misty haze, and interprets it as a cloud of passion: "as if the one hundred and twenty thousand souls had dispatched all at once the vapour of passions that she imagined in them." In the context of Flaubert's narrative structure, the haze bathing the town in the distance below constitutes an echo of the heroine's mental complexion. The fog is an equivalent of her melancholy, her ever-unsatisfied passion. The vertigo that she experiences looking at the city announces her eventual fall and her deception.

Such descriptions were no doubt familiar to Monet, who was an avid reader of Flaubert's novels. In an extraordinary letter to Alice Hoschedé, dated 30 April 1889 from the Creuse valley, Monet had written: "I am deep into examining my own canvases, that is, into pursuing my own torture. Well! If Flaubert had been a painter, what would he have written! for God's sake!"

The text that forms the most strikingly descriptive parallel to Monet's two 1892 views of Rouen can be read in *Bel-Ami*, whose author Guy de Maupassant had been well acquainted with Monet.

"Madeleine was tired and had dozed off, caressed by the bright rays of the sun which warmed her deliciously as she snuggled down in the old carriage, as though lying in a tepid bath full of life and country air.

"Her husband woke her up. 'Look', he said.

"They had just stopped two-thirds of the way up, at a spot well known for its view and visited by every tourist. They looked down on the immensely broad, long valley through which the glassy river flowed from one end to the other in sweeping curves. It could be seen coming from the distance, dotted with numerous islands and swinging round as it entered Rouen. Then on its right bank, slightly hazy in the morning mist, there appeared Rouen itself, its roofs gleaming in the sun and its hundreds of spires, slender, pointed or squat, frail and elaborate, like giant pieces of jewellery, its towers, square or round, crowned with armorial bearings, its belfries, its bell-towers, the whole host of Gothic church-tops dominated by the sharp-pointed spire of the cathedral, that sort of strange bronze needle, enormous, ugly and odd, the tallest in the world."

The thematic and visual kinships between Maupassant's text and Monet's two initial views of the cathedral spire in its urban

Vue de Rouen, Depuis La Côte Sainte-Catherine 1892, *Claude Monet, Private Collection*

surroundings are extremely revealing. Moreover, it is noteworthy that the neo-Gothic Viollet-le-Duc spire of the cathedral, "that sort of strange bronze needle, enormous, ugly and odd" was completely obliterated in Monet's *Cathedral* series. The most noticeable and the tallest feature of the cathedral, that Maupassant simply frowned upon and called "ugly", is the very feature that Monet chose to omit from the series paintings. The neo-Gothic spire is, however, quite noticeable in the first two paintings that Monet undertook during his visit to Rouen in 1892. These two paintings, together with *La Rue de l'Epicerie*, indicate that Monet did not have a definite notion of what he would do while in Rouen, or certainly cast a serious doubt on the hypothesis that Monet had already decided to tackle the cathedral before he set off for Rouen.[14]

Judging from the visual evidence of these three paintings alone, Monet was searching for a motif. He was looking initially at motifs that were heavily connotated and immediately recognizable, not only within the contemporary literary context but also within recent pictorial references to Rouen. This again refers us to Pissarro's 1883 trip to Rouen, from which he had returned with a harvest of prints and a completely refreshed source of pictorial subjects. However, it must be established that Pissarro's initial pictorial response to the city of Rouen was analogous but not necessarily similar to that of Monet.

The first analogy is a charcoal study by Pissarro, also entitled *View of Rouen*, in which Pissarro observed Rouen from above, from near the Côte Sainte-Catherine, offering a panoramic depiction of the city

Vue de Rouen 1883, Camille Pissarro, Musée du Louvre, Cabinet des Dessins, Paris

Vue de Rouen 1892, Claude Monet, Musée Marmottan, Paris

quite unusual in his gamut of motifs. This drawing and Monet's two paintings of 1892, both entitled *View of Rouen*, together with preparatory drawings for the paintings, feature the cathedral very centrally, prominently offset against the horizon line. It stands out against the sky, next to the smaller spire of the church of Saint-Maclou on the right of the drawing. A single common denominator to all these pictorial treatments of the cathedral within its surroundings is that the cathedral appears as dominating everything around it and is offset almost in isolation against an indefinable background.

The relevance of this drawing of Pissarro's within the initial context of Monet's *Cathedral* series can be further assessed through a letter from Pissarro to his son, dated 22 October 1883: "yesterday I was paid a visit by Monet, his brother and his son, by Durand-Ruel and his son. We spent the day together in Déville, on a high hill. There we saw the most splendid landscape that a painter could ever dream of: a view of Rouen, in the distance, with the Seine flowing, unfolding, as calm as a mirror, sunny slopes, splendid foregrounds: it was magical [*féérique*]. No doubt, I will go back to this village to paint there: it is marvellous."[15]

Pissarro did not go back, and never to our knowledge gave shape to this view, but there is little doubt that this text reveals the context of Pissarro's 1883 drawing, *View of Rouen*, and of Monet's treatment, twice in paint and twice in pencil, of the same subject matter nine years later. Pissarro and Monet discovered together the same panoramic and ecstatic view of Rouen, introduced to it by Monet's brother Léon, who lived nearby and knew the sites. There is more, however, in this central text: "splendid", "calm", "magical", "marvellous" – these are the terms used by Pissarro to describe this unique view of Rouen, and its cathedral featuring prominently above all and central to everything. It sets the mood for Monet's views of the same motif nine years later and, immediately following these, the *Cathedral* series.

Pissarro's text also introduces a notion that is vital to a more complete and fulfilling understanding of the Monet's *Cathedrals*: the word "*féérique*" (magical, or fairy-tale) is used to describe a view of Rouen which, in other words, looked unreal. The whole series of the *Cathedrals* brings this paradox to its climax and in a sense addresses, in most direct terms, the essential problem of pictorial and poetic creation. As G.H. Hamilton noted: "Here and there in the 1880s, in a letter to Durand-Ruel or in a remark of Pissarro's, we sense the difficulty Monet encountered in transforming the picture as the representation of something seen into a painting as an expressive work of art, that is to say, as a projection of his own inner sensibility, as a fact of consciousness rather than merely of observation."[16] Hamilton then further insists that the twenty paintings of Rouen Cathedral (then known in 1960 out of the thirty catalogued by Wildenstein) "are twenty episodes in the history of [Monet's] consciousness, and in thus substituting the 'laws of subjective experience for those of objective experience' he revealed a new psychic rather than physical reality."[17]

From the real to the unreal, from the objective to the subjective, from the "physical" to the "psychic", from the plain-spoken to the poetic or, in Pissarro's terms, from the "simple" to the "magical", this is the fragile equilibrium tantamount to artistic creation that Monet's *Cathedral* series revealed to its utmost.

This panoramic view of Rouen, which Maupassant found "touristic" and to which Léon Monet introduced Pissarro and Monet, probably thinking (and he was right) that it was a paintable subject, also caught Gauguin's interest. Gauguin, then very close to Pissarro, moved to Rouen on 1 November 1883 with the firm intention of setting off as a painter. In 1884, Gauguin produced his own version of the panoramic motif: in *Environs de Rouen* the cathedral

Environs de Rouen 1884, *Paul Gauguin, Sotheby's, London*

is there, pushed back to the left, with its recognizable, protruding, odd-looking spire. Gauguin's treatment of this almost inevitable motif is, however, more human in scale. The vantage point chosen by the artist is lower than in Pissarro's sketch or in Monet's two views of the subject. The cathedral is more tangible, less formidable. The presence of an odd isolated tree in the middle-ground increases this effect; the tree, appearing to compete in height with the spire that was known as "the tallest in the world", diminishes the importance of the cathedral. The cows in the foreground add to the awkwardness of the composition, with its wide-open perspective focusing nowhere in particular, and depicting too many things at the same time. This picture, for all its bizarre assemblage of discordant elements – the cathedral and the tree, the cows grazing in an open field – remains fascinating in the way that it almost seems to treat this well known, highly recognizable motif with irony.

It was most likely to this painting that Pissarro referred in a letter to Gauguin, written in the second half of May 1885, where he drew a sketch of Gauguin's painting depicting a church in a landscape at Rouen.[18] Pissarro harshly criticized the painting: "It is still a bit drab, the greens are not luminous enough." To which attack Gauguin immediately retorted, trying to defend himself with these words: "My Rouen series about which you speak is nothing but a passage or, instead, the base of that which I caught a glimpse of, that is, a very matt painting without apparent distance and the drab side doesn't scare me, feeling instead that it was necessary for me. I say necessary because, not having much experience and my art being more reflection than acquired skill, still I needed a point of departure opposed to the one which I hate in the painters who calculate their effects and show off."[19]

This text, where Gauguin defends his own clumsy version of the cathedral in its surroundings, is essential to a better understanding of the problems faced by Monet or Pissarro when confronted by Rouen. The dilemma was, to put it simply, either to do something "magical" or something calculated to "show off". This irresolvable problem might partly explain why Pissarro never produced a painted version of his pencil drawing and why Monet in 1892 might have felt unsatisfied with his initial beginnings of a series of a panoramic view of Rouen.

The last motif that Monet started to tackle, and left unfinished, was the *Rue de l'Epicerie*, with its two preparatory sketches. This motif equally enjoyed an extensive use within the context of Impressionist imagery of Rouen Cathedral. In this picture, left partly unresolved, Monet looked at the south entrance of the cathedral through the Rue de l'Epicerie that leads to the steps of the cathedral. Here we find another fertile ground on which to examine the constant dialogue between Monet and Camille Pissarro. Whereas

La Rue de l'Épicerie à Rouen 1892, *Claude Monet, Private Collection*

Pissarro exploited the motif of the Rue de l'Epicerie for a series of three paintings in 1898 (six years after Monet's series), he had already treated the same motif in a watercolour of 1883 (nine years before the *Cathedral* series). Pissarro produced the watercolour of this motif during his trip to Rouen in 1883, and then treated the Rue de l'Epicerie again in an etching. So, in this context, the history of this particular motif reads thus: Pissarro's watercolour, 1883; Pissarro's print, 1886; Monet's pencil sketches, 1892; Monet's painting, 1892; Pissarro's series of three paintings, 1898.

Again, and perhaps more so than other motifs, the Rue de l'Epicerie was ridden by other precedents. Every known motif tended to have been done and overdone by a previous tradition. Pissarro, in a letter to his son dated 20 November 1883, evokes this problem with a certain serenity, referring to a motif that he had just selected: "It is curious that Turner chose just this motif; one stumbles across the same places in Rouen. Yesterday I drew the Rue de Gros-Horloge; I have just seen, on leaving, a copy of the same place by Bonington from 1825 or '30."[20]

The Rue de l'Epicerie as a motif is no exception to this observation by Pissarro. It is a sort of roundabout of the Rouen iconography: one is bound to find somebody else who has done it before – "one stumbles across the same places". However, it really

La Rue de l'Épicerie à Rouen 1883, *Camille Pissarro, Private Collection*

did not seem to bother Pissarro or Monet to know that Rouen was swarming with past visual references.

Pissarro first sketched the motif of the Rue de l'Epicerie in watercolour in 1883 and the later etching was most likely done after this watercolour, since the layout of the two compositions is almost identical. The angle of Monet's view of 1892 is very close to both previous images by Pissarro, except that Monet stood a little further back from the cathedral and thus was able to depict more of the neo-Gothic spire (to the right in Monet's painting), whereas the same spire occupies only the upper right corner of Pissarro's watercolour and print. Monet's painting is the only known view of the cathedral that features the spire in close-up. It is also the only picture where Monet depicted the roof-top of the Tour Saint Romain, very recognizable in Monet's painting and also visible in Pissarro's watercolour and print. From then on, the Tour Saint Romain would be featured in every one of the thirty series paintings, but always truncated. The roof can never be seen, being too high for Monet's format, nor can the neo-Gothic spire, which remains hidden between the two western towers. The Tour de Beurre (the

south-west tower) cannot be seen in the pictures by Pissarro and Monet of the Rue de l'Epicerie: it is too far to the left of all three images. However, when Monet faces the west portal, the Tour de Beurre occasionally appears on the right-hand side of the picture.

From 1872 to 1892, the impressionistic treatment of the cathedral can be read as a fascinating multi-faceted visual dialogue between Pissarro and Monet. Both treated, at different times and in different ways, the same motifs. Both artists totally ignored the iconographic tradition of Rouen. Each was, however, highly aware of what the other was doing. After 1892, the split in their mutual subjects became quite radical. The last subject which they both treated was the Rue de l'Epicerie and the south portal of the cathedral. Monet left his painting unfinished, Pissarro developed the subject into a series in 1898. When Monet chose to paint the west portal of the cathedral, he was alone. Pissarro had never treated that motif, and never did.

In this sense, Monet's *Cathedral* series constitutes a radical break with Impressionism, conceived as a common corpus of visual concerns treated by different individuals. The *Cathedral* series cuts Monet's ties with Impressionism and with Camille Pissarro, in a way that had previously been indicated in the progression of his work, but not quite achieved.

La Rue de l'Épicerie à Rouen 1886, *Camille Pissarro, British Museum, London*

MONET IN FRONT OF THE CATHEDRAL

Monet's visit to Rouen in 1892 was occasioned by family business relating to his half-sister Marie, who had died in 1891. Marie was the child of a liaison between Monet's father, Adolphe Monet, and the family maid that had begun after the death of Claude and Léon's mother in 1857. Marie was twenty years younger than Claude Monet, and had only been registered as a legitimate child by Monet's father when he eventually consented to marry Marie's mother in 1870: the little girl was then ten years old. When Adolphe Monet died in 1871, the heritage was divided into three equal shares between the two brothers and their half-sister. It included an impressive array of Claude Monet's paintings, which the artist would undoubtedly have preferred to have been returned to his own studio. Both brothers certainly resented the intrusion of a much younger half-sister whom they hardly knew, but the equal inheritance was upheld in French law with the result that Marie received a one-third share of the paintings that had belonged to Monet's father.

These paintings were obviously of quality and significance to Monet's eye. Pissarro later attested to this in clear terms, in a letter written to his son Lucien from Rouen in 1883: "I had dinner with Monet's brother in Déville-les-Rouen; he showed me paintings by Monet and smaller works by Renoir that are superb!"

After Marie's sudden death, Monet and his brother were quite keen to repossess their half-sister's share of their father's legacy. They arranged to buy back Marie's heritage from her mother who, not being informed about the suddenly high prices fetched by Monet's paintings, agreed to sell for a very reasonable sum the pictures that had belonged to Marie. Their business completed, Léon invited Claude Monet to return with him to Déville for a family visit. Monet, however, was careful not to let personal matters override his need to get back to work and, rather than stay at Léon's home, he took a room at the Hôtel d'Angleterre in Rouen, not far from the cathedral. From here he went out in search of a motif and, as we have seen, began work with the two panoramic views of Rouen and the view onto the south side of the cathedral through the Rue de l'Epicerie. Finally, as if naturally completing the progression towards the motif previously described, Monet stood directly in front of the cathedral.

What transpires clearly from Monet's first letters from Rouen, and from the first works executed there in 1892, is that the *Cathedral* series was not a premeditated project. The first letter written from Rouen that has survived was sent by Monet to his wife-to-be Alice Hoschedé, on Friday 12 February 1892. In this letter Monet informed Alice of his prompt return to Giverny. The letter also indicates that Monet had already been in Rouen for a while – at least a few days – and that he was not getting on as he had hoped: "It is really not my thing to live in cities and I am bored stiff, all the more as this is not working out as I wish." The dissatisfaction thus expressed is reflected by the fact that of the first three paintings started in and around Rouen, two were left unfinished, and that for each motif Monet resorted to one or more pencil sketches.

Among the first works that Monet painted once he began to focus closely on the cathedral as his motif are two astonishing views of the Tour Saint Romain, the north-west tower of the cathedral (Plates 1 and 2). These can be singled out from the main groups of paintings forming the *Cathedral* series primarily for their subject matter, in that all other paintings in the series focus on the western façade of the cathedral. There are two other important differences: the pictures of the Tour Saint Romain were painted outdoors; furthermore, Monet

LEFT La Cour d'Albane 1892, *Claude Monet, Musée Marmottan, Paris*
RIGHT Le Portail, La Cathédrale de Rouen 1892, *Claude Monet, Musée Marmottan, Paris*

was working at ground level and, as a result, could only encompass the lower part of the tower within his range of vision. Despite these differences, Monet clearly felt that these pictures were part of the whole series, since they were included in the 1895 exhibition where the *Cathedrals* were first publicly shown.

In his letter of 12 February, Monet also expressed a vague sigh of relief. After having run around the city in search of a motif, after suffering from the cold while working in the open air, Monet dared to voice some contentment: "I am nevertheless a bit happier today, I was able to install myself in an empty apartment facing the Cathedral, but it is a tough job that I am undertaking here." Monet had finally found his spot, and there began work on the *Cathedral* series as we know it.

Out of his newly found location, Monet started to paint the first two views of the western façade (plates 3 and 4). It appears that this is all he had time for, since Monet's letter informing Alice that he had found a proper location facing the cathedral also warned her that he would be returning home to Giverny the next day (Saturday 13 February). In effect, Monet had only two days, or more likely a day and a half, in which to undertake these two views which both offer the same singularly frontal view of the cathedral's western façade. Having decided to grapple with the cathedral directly, Monet did so in a very forthright manner.

Both of these frontal views are clearly recognizable from the fact that they show the widest gap between the left tower and the central section of the façade. These are also the only two views in which the base of the neo-Gothic central spire is visible. This spire, a late addition to the cathedral architecture, appears in almost every single traditional view of the cathedral, and in all previous depictions by Monet, Pissarro or Gauguin. The spire becomes all the more conspicuous by its absence from Monet's series, since he clearly decided to omit it from his paintings after these first two views.

Monet most certainly decided to return home to spend Sunday with his adopted family in Giverny. He took ill, however, and therefore had to delay his plans to return to his work site in Rouen. The following Sunday, he wrote a semi-apologetic letter to Durand-Ruel, which is interestingly vague about what he had been doing: "You presumably imagine me in the midst of intense work in Rouen. Indeed I was there and had undertaken several things, but I have been kept sick here for a whole week." These several things obviously refer to everything that Monet had done thus far: his two panoramic views, his Rue de l'Epicerie, probably at least the beginnings of his two Tour Saint Romain paintings, and the first two frontal views of the cathedral. Monet must have felt that there was not quite enough to boast about, nor enough views of a single motif to be called a series.

If Monet, according to his letter to Alice, left Rouen for Giverny on 13 February, it was not until 25 February that he was back in Rouen. Monet's mind was also kept busy by the organization of his *Poplars* exhibition at Durand-Ruel's gallery. He had promised Durand-Ruel that he would come to the gallery the following Monday (29 February) to hang the paintings. Monet spent a lot of time during that period commuting between Rouen, Giverny and Paris.

On his return to the cathedral, Monet had to face the disappointment of finding the room that he had previously used as a studio now occupied by workers who were resurfacing the floor. He therefore had to settle in another room, which he found at the opposite corner of the same block, a few numbers south of his first location. Monet actually moved from the north-west end of the block to the south-west end, from number 31 Place de la Cathédrale to number 23. Despite this revision to his plans, Monet appeared to be in optimistic mood when he resumed work on the *Cathedral* paintings, and his letters subsequently show that the displacement was temporary. As soon as the workers had finished the floor at number 31, a few days later, Monet was able to resume painting there, as well as continuing work at number 23. In fact, as will be explained, he divided his time quite methodically between the two locations during the rest of his stay in Rouen in 1892.

The question of the exact dating of each *Cathedral* is an almost impossible one to resolve since, as we know, they were all considerably reworked by the time they were "finished" and dated in 1894. It is tempting, however, to establish approximate dates according to the vantage point depicted in each work, as Daniel Wildenstein does in his *Catalogue Raisonné* of Monet's work. Leaving aside the two views of the Tour Saint Romain, all the twenty-eight remaining *Cathedrals* were executed from three different locations. This is how one can read the successive steps of Monet's series:

1. *Chez* M. Jean Louvet, "*la grande fabrique*", 31 Place de la Cathédrale, at the corner of the Rue du Gros-Horloge. This was the location offering the most frontal view of the cathedral, the "empty apartment" described in Monet's letter of 12 February 1892, where he began the first two views of the western façade. He returned to the Louvet house during his 1892 visit, and again in 1893,[1] although in 1892 he was on two occasions interrupted by workers refurbishing the apartment.

2. *Chez* M. Fernand Lévy, "*Boutique de lingerie et modes*", 23 Place de la Cathédrale, at the corner of the Rue du Petit-Salut (now called Rue Ampère). Previously this was the site of the Bureau of Finance that had been depicted in part by J.M.W. Turner in his *Rivers of France*. Monet worked at this location from his return from Giverny on 25 February 1892 until mid-April of the same year.

3. *Chez* M. Edouard Mauquit, "*Le magasin de nouveautés*", 81 Rue du Grand-Pont (now number 47). This location, very close to M. Lévy's boutique, was used between mid-February and mid-April 1893.[2]

It is interesting to attempt to answer the question of which paintings were executed in which location. We can establish that the first location, the Louvet house, provides the most frontal approach to the cathedral, as evidenced in plates 3 and 4, paintings almost certainly begun at Louvet's on 12 and 13 February 1892. Since Monet used the same house, although not necessarily the same window or the same orientation on the cathedral façade, later in his 1892 stay in Rouen and again in 1893, the question then is, which are the paintings, apart from the two already cited, that offer the most frontal view of the cathedral? The viewpoint closest to these two original views is clearly the one portrayed in plates 5 to 13, which also offer two gaps of sky that can be seen between the central portal of the cathedral and the two flanking towers. The gaps of sky are large and visible in the first two paintings, but less conspicuous in the group of nine paintings, later on painted from the Louvet house. In these, the gap on the left has become more like a thin, vertical sliver. There remains the question of whether all of these nine paintings were begun during the return to Louvet's in 1892.

The progression from location one, the Louvet house, to location three, Mauquit's shop, is one from left to right as one faces the cathedral or, equally, from north to south. Progressing to the right, one has to turn gradually more to the left in order to keep the cathedral in focus. From Mauquit's, furthest to the right, one could have seen, looking left, the houses attached to the left of the Tour Saint Romain. These houses were destroyed during World War II, as was the *établissement* Mauquit. The vantage point that can be experienced today from the building that has replaced Mauquit's shop is very similar to the vantage point depicted in plates 25 to 30. These are the only views in which the Tour Saint Romain can be seen in its whole width. Correspondingly, the Tour de Beurre, the tower partly seen on the right of the west portal, had to be omitted from these views.

By deduction, one can assume that the paintings executed in location two, Lévy's boutique, are plates 14 to 24. The second and third locations were only separated by the tiny Rue Ampère (as it is called today), whose name hardly even appears on maps of Rouen. Being so close, the Lévy and Mauquit sites offered Monet similar vantage points, the first in 1892, the second in 1893. Thus the chronological progression of the *Cathedral* series can be broadly reconstructed as follows:

1. Two paintings, plates 3 and 4, were begun at the Louvet house on 12 and 13 February 1892.

2. On his return to Rouen in late February 1892, after recovering from illness at Giverny, Monet started work at Lévy's boutique on a group that finally consisted of eleven paintings, plates 14 to 24.

3. During the same period in 1892, Monet went back to work at the Louvet house as soon as his room was cleared by the workers. There, as can be found from evidence in Monet's letters, he worked on paintings depicting late afternoon and evening effects. Five of the paintings are clearly identifiable as such: plates 8 to 12.

4. In 1893, Monet again used two locations – the Louvet house for the second time, and Mauquit's shop. From the Louvet house in 1893 he obviously reworked his late afternoon and evening paintings of the year before, and most probably started other paintings which show early afternoon effects – plates 5, 6 and 7.

5. At Mauquit's in 1893, Monet reworked some morning effects executed at Lévy's boutique in 1892 (as explained to Alice in a letter written on 16 February 1893) and also started six new canvases, all morning effects. These were plates 25 to 30.

In order to classify the paintings within each of the groups, it is useful to refer to Monet's frequent correspondence with Alice, in which he reports the changes in the weather with the regularity of a weather forecast. Two parameters enter into the classification of each painting – the time and the weather. It is interesting to note here that the French word *temps* covers both notions. Indeed, the complication is that time and weather are intricately interwoven with each other. Occasionally, the weather completely disguises the time: no matter what the time of day, the light is grey and dirty. On other occasions the time moves too fast to record the limpid weather.

On his return to Rouen on 25 February 1892, starting to use the new location at Lévy's boutique, Monet wrote as usual to Alice in the evening and was elated about the weather. The letter begins: "I have arrived here with superb weather". Soon after lunch with his brother, Monet went straight to work, as he explained to Alice, "at my window where I am comfortably seated. The Cathedral in the sun is admirable. I started two of them". As the letter continued, the weather assumed even more importance: "The beautiful weather goes on, I am happy, but, damn, what a job that Cathedral. It is terrible, and I do hope not to have too many changes of weather." The weather totally conditions Monet's working time and his schedule. His letter goes on: "If the weather turns bad, I will come back during the day". We understand from this that Monet meant to return to Giverny for the weekend, leaving early if conditions were unfavourable; but that if the weather stayed fine, he would not leave Rouen until evening in order not to waste the daylight hours that he needed for his work.

The information in this letter contributes to the attempt to identify the progress of each group of paintings in the *Cathedral* series. Monet reports that the first two paintings from Lévy's were begun after he had lunched with his brother, and that the weather was "superb". There are two paintings in the Lévy group that reflect this glowing weather, and that represent early afternoon light, judging from the thin, minimal shadow that is starting to grow obliquely. These two paintings are Plates 21 and 22. One of these is the first painting of this newly emerging series. The second one must have been started as the afternoon wore on. The two paintings from the same location that show excellent weather conditions and mid-afternoon light, from perhaps 2 to 3pm, are Plates 23 and 24.

Monet's next letter to Alice was written on 8 March from Rouen, after he had, in the meantime, made a trip to Paris to hang his *Poplars* exhibition at Durand-Ruel's. In this letter Monet again mentions the weather – a fundamental concern of his pictorial pursuits: "I am still keeping well and I see clearly through what I am doing: it will probably be all right if the sun lasts, but I am rather afraid as I have just seen the moon surrounded with a huge double circle, which foretells nothing good." This letter offers a fascinating mine of details about Monet's approach, his anxieties and concerns, his ambition in respect to the cathedral. It includes his explanation to Alice of his refusal to succumb to the pressing demand of the Rouen collector Depeaux to acquire two *Cathedrals*, one for Depeaux himself and one for the museum in Rouen. Monet is categorical on this point, that he must work through all the paintings before any are released, in order to have "seen them and seen them again in Giverny".

At the same time, Monet had to face a personal dilemma: he would either satisfy Alice's regular request to have him return home, or he would keep at his *Cathedrals*. He opted for the latter, using the weather as an explanation: "I want very much to come to Giverny, but even so, I have to stay as long as the sun will last." This, depending upon how one might interpret it, could have meant an eternity. But Monet gently explained, "for afterwards the sun will remain hidden for a long time, I am afraid". The conclusion of Monet's letter to Alice carries little romanticism: "Otherwise I have not many things to tell you; I dig hard, I strive a lot and I think only about my *Cathedrals*. I am going back to look at them for an hour, while I smoke my pipe, and before going to bed: indeed, I get up early: at 8am I am at my shopkeeper's."

On 9 March, we learn from a letter to Durand-Ruel, "the weather is turning bad". Monet is disturbed by the bad weather, and even proposes "to take advantage of it and to go and spend a day in Giverny". This seems to indicate that in this early stage of his series, Monet did not care to paint the cathedral under the effects of poor weather conditions.

On the following day, 10 March, Monet wrote an enraged letter to Alice after reading the news that Suzanne Hoschedé, one of Alice's daughters, wished to marry the American painter Theodore Butler. Monet warned Alice: "It is your duty to refuse your daughter to an American, unless he is known to us through a contact or through an introduction, not someone met on the road." In order to resolve this sudden family crisis, Monet returned to Giverny. In fact, the crisis eventually found a happy resolution. For in the summer of the same year (1892), shortly after having finished his first campaign on the *Cathedral* series, Monet proudly accompanied his stepdaughter Suzanne to the altar of the church in Giverny for her marriage to Theodore Butler. A few weeks beforehand, Monet himself had been to the same altar for another wedding: his own to Alice Hoschedé. Thereby Monet had made official his union with the future bride's mother. After first receiving the news of Suzanne's engagement in March, however, the situation probably felt too tense and too novel to be accepted immediately. Monet's visit to Giverny enabled him to iron out the problems and make plans for the summer; he then returned to Rouen.

Writing to Alice on 18 March, Monet gave some information that again proves useful to the study of his working method and the sequence of the series paintings. He explained that he had been caught by his brother Léon as he was leaving work at about 7pm, and was persuaded to have dinner with Léon and few colleagues. We now know that Monet's working day lasted from 8am (letter of 8 March) until 6 or 6:30pm (letter of 18 March). Assuming that Monet took an hour for lunch, it meant that he worked steadily for 10 hours. Another crucial detail is found in the 18 March letter: "I worked like a slave," he wrote, "today nine canvases". This implies that Monet was at that time working on one canvas per hour, approximately. "You can imagine how tired I am," Monet's letter continued, "but I am amazed with Rouen, with all that one could do here. I do not know how I shall get out of it this time; in any case, I am trying very hard." Mention is again made of the weather, which is still beautiful, and of the fact that Monet would find it imprudent to leave the cathedral and return to Giverny while the weather remained so good.

The next letter to Alice, written on 26 March, brings a halt to this period of emphasis on the favourable conditions for Monet's work. Monet first thanked Alice for her consoling lines, but complained that a wasted day can never be regained. He had feared that the weather would be even worse than it was, but admitted that he was "able to work on two canvases of bad weather". He also gave a precious indication about Plates 1 and 2, the views of the Tour Saint Romain: because of a bad cold, he did not wish to risk working outdoors in the cathedral backyard. Either he had previously made a start on the outdoor views and felt that they needed further work, or he had conceived the idea of these unusual paintings but put off starting work until recovered from his cold.

Predictably, since the weather had turned bad, even terrible (Monet described a storm with bolts of lightning), he became available to return to Giverny for a traditional Sunday lunch with the family. From then on, back in Rouen, it seemed that the situation went from bad to worse. In a letter written on 30 March in reply to one from Alice, Monet was near despair: "Yes, we have the same weather here, a terrible cold and wind, and I assure you that I need some courage to carry on." "I have looked at my sunny motifs again: two of them are unretouchable – therefore completed. The others need to be more or less adjusted." This is a crucial observation, since it indicates that Monet may have completed certain paintings on the spot, in front of the cathedral, and that not all of the paintings need have been reworked later in his studio at Giverny.

In the next letter to Alice, dated 31 March, the crisis had reached a climax: "Tonight I am worn out, as my writing will show. I have transformed, destroyed all my sunny canvases; fate has decided, I must admit there are a few that I must regret. If the good weather goes on, I may be able to work it through; but if I am interrupted again I will limit myself to finishing my two or three grey weathers; but how can one predict?"

However, this letter ends up on a more positive note and indicates clearly that the series to date was far from "destroyed": "I believe in the good weather, if such is the case, I will do the impossible and it will work (…) I am now going to go to my bedroom and meditate on today's work. (…) Depeaux came to see me again yesterday evening and brought me an excellent gas lantern with a projector. I can view my canvases admirably."

The next letter, dated 2 April, only confirms the rather dramatic, albeit quite positive changes undertaken: "I am worn out, I have never been so exhausted physically and morally; it has driven me silly and I only want my bed; but I am glad, very glad, and will become even gladder if this marvellous weather lasts a few more days. At last, I feel that I will bring back something, but will I have that stroke of luck? The barometer is going down slightly." The letter includes one more detail of Monet's schedule: "Imagine that I get up before 6am and at work from 7am until 6.30 in the evening, always standing – nine canvases. It is killing, and for this matter I abandon everything, you, my garden."

Another incident had surfaced to stain Monet's new wave of optimism. The shopkeeper, M. Lévy, had asked Monet not to work on his premises, explaining that his lady clients were somewhat disturbed. It is understandable that the ladies might have been reluctant to try on new garments in the presence of that awesome, shaggy-bearded figure painting away in the corner of the shop. Monet had to double or triple his daily rent in order to be tolerated by the shopkeeper.

The following day, a Sunday, Monet was pining for a letter from Alice and for Giverny. He described the weather as "unheard of" and "too beautiful, alas, to last". He anxiously watched the barometer decline, but was able to report: "In brief, another excellent day, every day I add and catch something new that I had not been able to see before." This letter of 3 April continued on an extremely optimistic note, confirming that the paintings referred to previously had not been irremediably spoiled: "What a difficulty, but it is working; a few more days of this gorgeous sun, and a good number of my canvases will be salvaged." We understand here that his description of the earlier crisis – "I have destroyed all my sunny canvases" – most probably meant that Monet had reworked them unsatisfactorily, rather than done them physical and irretrievable damage. These paintings were now in the process of being rescued.

Although things had improved during the day, there had been a crisis of quite a different kind. In the same letter Monet described a most extraordinary event: "This usually never happens to me, I slept a night filled with nightmares: the Cathedral would crash on top of me, it would appear either blue or pink or yellow." This text seems of great significance, pointing out that Monet's range of imaginative forces was at work on his *Cathedrals* day and night, within a vastly complex task in which the conscious and unconscious both played their roles. It prompts us as viewers, if we had not been convinced of it already, to look at Monet's *Cathedral* series as something less simple less straightforward than a merely realistic account of the changes of light on a stone façade.

On a more mundane level, Monet's letter explains that the embarrassment his presence had caused to the female clientele in the shop where he worked has been resolved. Depeaux had brought him a screen behind which he could hide and paint away. Thus the modesty of the ladies of Rouen would be kept intact, while Monet could continue work.

A short note followed the next day (4 April): "Still beautiful weather – it works very well. But the wind has turned to the west, I am afraid, still – another three or four days and my main ones will be salvaged." In another telegraphic-style note (5 April), we find a useful mention of the time of his lunch break: "If the sun is up, I have lunch at 11am as I have to be back at work from 12 to 2pm." Indeed, the line of shadow in the works that can be identified as from this period indicates that a few of the canvases were painted around midday, such as Plates 19, 20 and 21 (between 12 noon and 1pm) and Plate 22 (probably painted between 1 and 2pm), which was obviously a time of day when Monet worked with particular intensity.

These timings refer to the paintings in the Lévy group of 1892. However, it is apparent that at some time during the main period of his stay in Rouen, Monet had been able to return to work at the Louvet house, his first location which he had had to abandon in late February while the apartment was being refurbished. In a letter written on 7 April, we find a very important piece of information with regard to his use of the two locations, which echoes the problem he had previously faced in respect of the Louvet house. Monet wrote to Alice: "I continued my work with zeal, but a disappointment was about to come in the evening for the two red and gold motifs: I was refused access to the so-called house because the architect had left orders with the painters not to let me in, and that I must hand back the keys to the architect. You can imagine my frustration, with such weather, so that since 4pm I have not been doing anything."

From this we understand how methodical was the routine that Monet applied to the *Cathedral* paintings in 1892. Monet painted in the mornings at Lévy's boutique, and worked there until 3 or 3.30pm. He then moved to the Louvet house for a second session of work, on different canvases, that lasted from about 4 to 7pm. In this instance, because of the architect who kept the keys to the apartment at Louvet's, Monet had wasted three hours of solid, good weather. Monet decided to act upon the matter immediately, so that his next afternoon should not also be wasted. "I went to Depeaux's without seeing him, and then to the *Nouvelliste* [the offices of a newspaper] where Lapierre lent his help to go and find someone on very good terms with the architect, so that it will be explained [to him] what harm he has done to me, and so that I may be able to work tomorrow. Clearly, it is not just the poplars that give me trouble, and it really is tough to have fine weather and not to be able to take advantage of it."[3]

Despite these few incidents, the spring of 1892 was unusually beautiful, as can be seen from a glance at the paintings that Monet initiated through March and April. Alice was again pressing Monet to return to Giverny. Monet's answer, dated 9 April, set his priorities as usual: "I wish I could tell you that I am coming tomorrow, but despite my wish and my need to come to Giverny, at the point where I am, I have to do everything to lead my canvases to a final result. I have an amazing fluke with this weather, but I have now caught such a peculiar way of working that, whatever I may do, I do not seem to progress very far; furthermore, everyday I discover things unseen the day before – I add and I lose certain things. Well, indeed I am searching for the impossible. In a nutshell, I will only come tomorrow if the weather should get worse toward the evening, and so I have to think about my morning canvases on Monday! What a system! I have to be caught deep in it not to come. Well, maybe I will come, but nothing is less certain."

On 12 and 13 April 1892, Monet was still in Rouen, from where he wrote letters to his dealer before finally returning to Giverny. Besides asking for money to be sent or transferred, Monet always seemed to be complaining to Durand-Ruel: "I am as always at work, for despite this superb weather, I am not happy at all and I wish I had not wasted so much time here." (12 April) "I am completely discouraged and unhappy with what I have done here, I have tried to perfect it too far and have only managed to spoil what was good. For the last four days I have not been able to work and so I have decided to give up everything and to go back home. But I do not even want to unpack my canvases there; I only want to see them after some while. I will let you know when I feel a little more relaxed." (13 April)

Monet spent the whole summer, the autumn and some of the winter at Giverny. He married Alice, and witnessed the marriage of Alice's daughter Suzanne. Meanwhile, despite some less than cooperative behaviour towards his dealer, Monet gradually came to the idea of showing his "Rouen endeavours" although, as he had reiterated in a letter to Durand-Ruel of 11 May 1892, he remained "quite determined not to sell any of them". Toward the end of 1892, Monet tried to find a pretext for not showing any work to the dealer, and the subject of laziness surfaced when he wrote to Durand-Ruel on 28 October: "I will be very happy to see you, but unfortunately I have nothing to show you. This year I have been totally lazy, which frightens me a bit, I must admit. You will scold me, and you will do the right thing, as this will give me some courage." Indeed, Monet probably was rather slow during that year. In all, only fifteen canvases can be counted between his departure from Rouen in mid-April 1892 and his return there in mid-February 1893.

As soon as he returned to Rouen, Monet felt like a fish in water. Unable to use Lévy's premises, he had to find a replacement – the Mauquit shop, separated from Lévy's only by the tiny Rue Grand-Pont, running between them. Monet again had a direct viewpoint onto the western façade of the cathedral very similar to that of the year before.

In his first letter to Alice from Rouen in 1893, on 16 February, Monet seemed at ease and knew exactly what he was after: "I have not wasted any time since I arrived. As soon as I took a room, my luggage stowed, I went to the Rue Grand-Pont; the installation is very good and the workers had just finished. Having done that, I went to M. Louvet's to ask for the keys of the big house: I had somebody carry easels into these two places and this morning I was back at work."

The previous year, Monet had initiated at least six "gold and red" motifs (plates 8 to 12) and one grey weather (plate 13), and certainly his two initial frontal views (plates 3 and 4): altogether at least nine paintings from Louvet's. At Lévy's he had begun eleven paintings (plates 14 to 24), which is explainable by the fact that he had been relatively less disturbed there than at Louvet's and had spent a greater span of time there on each working day.

The main object of the second sojourn in front of the cathedral was, principally, to strive to lead these 20 or more paintings to a conclusion and, of course, to experiment with a few more views. The new venue at Mauquit's *magasin de nouveautés*, although very close to Lévy's boutique, was slightly further down to the right, or south of the cathedral. The view is angled more to the left of the cathedral, hence the attached row of houses visible in plates 25 to 30, which are unlike any of Monet's motifs of the previous year. Mauquit's venue was, however, close enough to allow Monet to rework the Lévy paintings without any problems: "I have started two paintings and here I am deep into my subject. By working this way, when I see my last year's effects to the point of coming, I will be able to work at it shortly." (16 February 1893)[4]

Monet at first seemed supremely confident: "Here is what will please you: I am hopeful of coming out victorious from all this work." Of course, he had only just started again on the series, and soon the traditional dialogue of the previous year was to resume. To Alice's request to visit him in Rouen, Monet retorted: "I find that the first thing to think about is work; I had too much disappointment last year." In a postscript to this letter of 20 February 1893, Monet added: "Your visit would puzzle me at this point when I absolutely need all my willpower and all my strengths to go through this vast difficulty."

Monet reverted to familiar habits. A letter of 21 February mentions that he was again accustomed to take a break for lunch at 11am and was leading "a regular and tranquil life". Then followed the indispensable observations on the weather: "I have managed to work, though not without trying hard and having many interruptions because of the weather. At some moments during the day, it was impossible to see through." The weather remained bad for a while, but the most important change was one in Monet's working method. He started fewer works and consolidated intensely those begun the previous year: "Since I arrived here a week ago tomorrow, I have worked on the same two canvases every day, and I cannot reach what I want; oh well! it will come out of continuously trying so hard." (22 February 1893)

As the overcast conditions continued, Monet was able to work out his various grey weather paintings: "A grey, filthy, slightly misty weather is still up, which helps me fine, but even though I do some good, long sessions, it progresses very slowly. What a complication, that work!" (24 February 1893) The feeling of slow progress or no progress at all became worse in the course of time: "I am furious with myself: I do nothing good. There we are: I do not know how many sessions I spend on these canvases, and with all this effort, it goes nowhere, I am groping and not at all doing what I want; it is heartbreaking." Necessarily, the process of completing a painting was a far more tedious and time-consuming task than the more immediately rewarding job of sketching the transient and fleeting effect of a particular motif.

In a letter written on 3 March 1893, Monet integrated all the fundamental concerns that he faced in the making of the *Cathedrals*: the time it was taking to work through the series; the strength and formidable work that he needed to achieve his ambition; the question of time in general – in essence, Monet's own finite time offset against the cathedral's "eternal" time; the weather conditions; the changing duration of the sunlight as the season evolved.

Nevertheless, the letter expresses a certain respite: "Today it has been a little better and I will get through with that Cathedral, but I need a lot of time. It will only be through obstinate work that I will manage what I want; it would actually not be that surprising that this time might not be the end of it and that I might have to come back next year. I will of course do everything I can to get through it this time: this will depend on the weather. At any rate, I do not want to stay at it for an eternity, nor do I want to transform my canvases gradually as the sun will be getting higher".

More details are found in each letter and one feels that, as Monet pointed out, had he stayed there for an eternity he would see something different every day. On 7 March, another observation was made about the weather that allows us tentatively to identify a few of the *Cathedrals*: "Today has been very beautiful, grey and sunny, and in the morning, mist; as a result I got up very early and was at work at 7.15. I am very tired as I have worked on eight different canvases, at which I am glancing as I write to you." These canvases could be those shown in plates 14, 19 and 20, and the few with houses attached.

The weather turned to Monet's liking; it became superb. Predictably, then, Monet renounced returning to Giverny. However, these moments of relative contentment and optimism, particularly in 1893, appear like a short-lived sunny spell in spring and a few days later Monet's mood returned to its sullen, glum self: "I am digging like a madman, but alas, you may all say what you will, I emptied my bag and am no longer good for anything."

This letter of 9 March reflects a deeply morose state, to the extent that Monet felt he could not answer a pleasant letter from his favourite stepdaughter, Blanche, because he saw everything in black. Although very depressive, the letter offers a fascinating account of Monet's psychological complexion with regard to his work, together with a very interesting comparison between his work of 1892 and of 1893: "Everything goes at the same time – the weather is not very regular: yesterday – splendid sun; this morning – fog; in the afternoon – sun again, that just went when I needed it; tomorrow it will be grey-black or rain, and I am very afraid, yet again, of dropping it and of coming back all of a sudden (...) Even though I am working, I am getting nowhere. This evening, I wanted to compare what I have done with my old canvases, which I am trying to keep out of sight in order not to fall into the same mistakes. Well! The result is that I am quite right to have been dissatisfied last year: it is horrible and what I am doing this time is just as bad, bad in a different way, that is all."

Monet continued this extraordinary letter to Alice, who must have wondered how to pull her husband out of this terrible depression. Finally, Monet ventured a solution to the problem, a solution that had to do with making use of time, while experiencing and dealing with its effects: "One should not want to work that fast, to try and try again, in order to do it again a final time. (...) But I feel that I am becoming weary; I am at the end of my tether; and this proves clearly that I have completely emptied my bag. (...) My goodness! they are not very far-sighted, those who see a master in me! Beautiful intentions, yes, but that's it! Happy the younger ones, those who believe that it is easy; I was like that once, but it is over; yet tomorrow morning at 7.00 I'll be there." This very moving document reveals, among other features, that Monet in the depth of his depression and self-deprecation will nonetheless recover himself and doggedly continue with his work.

The following week, on 14 March, Monet wrote to Durand-Ruel. His letter explains that things had not evolved: "I have been here for a month and it does not get anywhere. My work feels more and more like heavy going. On top of this – miserable weather. I would need a whole week of sunshine." This letter repeats the depressive tone, but allows us to perceive how and in what state of mind Monet progressed in his work. It also reveals an interesting detail about the frames Monet used at the time. The artist required some frames from Durand-Ruel for an exhibition of his works in London: "are they white or gilded?" is his question to Durand-Ruel, suggesting that most of the frames he used were one or the other. It is tempting in this context to imagine how an exhibition of twenty *Cathedrals* in white frames would have looked.

In a letter to Alice the next day, 15 March, Monet wrote: "This Cathedral is admirable, but it is terribly dry and tough to do. It will be sheer delight for me, after this, to paint outdoors." It seems that Monet was as unlucky with the weather in 1893 – grey and miserable most of the time – as he had been lucky in 1892. "The days succeed each other and all look alike, alas," he complained in his letter of 16 March. "If only I had some good weather," he continued, "it seems to me that with all these efforts, all this research, I could manage – but with the weather here, it is impossible; and yet, I am struggling and working all the same, dropping and taking back my canvases as the time and/or the weather changes; it drives me silly and is very tiring." The description Monet gave of the weather on 17 March sounds almost unreal: "This morning there was superb weather, but it was very short-lived. At 9am: hailstorms; and all the day has been a sequence of rain, snow, sunshine every ten minutes, real downpour-ings and quite cold." It sounds as if the weather itself intended to trick Monet at his own game and to make it impossible for him to follow the wild succession of variations it imposed.

Monet's fortune started to be served when 20 March turned out a fine spring day: "What a beautiful day, and also, what nice work I have got through. I have been working since this morning, without a break until after 6pm – nine canvases. But I am tired and only wish to be in bed. If only I could have this weather for a couple of weeks, that would be very pleasing." On 21 March, Monet again rejoiced over the "admirable weather". He was applying himself with great concentration and found no time to look back over his work. He seemed optimistic, though enormously tired, complaining on 23 March that he had worked so hard, his thumb was painful and swollen from holding his palette.

It seems that Monet was working on more canvases simultaneously than ever before. Of course, several of these canvases were paintings that he had begun the year before. Whereas in 1892, Monet had worked on about nine paintings in one day, which in itself is a good average, in 1893 he expected to average twelve a day. On 23 March a local event slightly disturbed his output. A monument to the memory of Archbishop Bonnechose was being inaugurated and a black mourning veil was stretched across the cathedral portal. Consequent-ly, Monet worked on only ten paintings that day. He received an invitation to the memorial mass, with a choir of 300 performers, which he found "marvellously beautiful" as he was, moreover, "admirably seated". His ear for sacred music did not tone down the sharpness of his eye, however: "I saw superb things to do inside, and I only wish that I had seen them earlier (...) In short, it was a very beautiful concert in an admirable context."[5]

The weather remained unusually satisfactory until 30 March. At last, Monet found himself able to follow the progression of his studies of the previous year. Extraordinarily, Monet seemed still unsatisfied. He wrote on 24 March that if the superb weather "should last all the time, I should pray that it might stop, or otherwise I should stop myself, unless I could begin new canvases all the time." A few days later (29 March), Monet described himself as a "prisoner" of his Cathedrals, which he explained thus: "I have to get through to the end although, in fact, I am nearly at the end of my tether; it is a job that is killing me and I work with feverish enthusiasm." He broke his record that day, working on fourteen canvases: "Never has such a thing happened to me," Monet boasted.

Monet necessarily felt that he had made some progress; he was now less than two weeks away from returning home and felt somewhat anxious to be back in Giverny, as can be sensed from his letters. It is, however, worth quoting again from his letter to Alice of 29 March in order to understand the new types of problems that he faced as he came nearer to completing his series. "If I lived in Rouen," he wrote, "it is only now that I would start to understand my subject. It took me time but I am near the end, and my stay here will not last much longer; first of all because I am too exhausted and obsessed with the idea of going back, and because it [the light] changes in a huge way. It is no longer the oblique light of the February days; it is every day more white, more vertical, and as early as tomorrow I am going to work on two or three extra canvases." Two weeks or so before leaving Rouen for good Monet, under the impact of the ceaseless change of light, felt compelled to start on new canvases to take account of that white, darting, vertical sunlight: ceaseless variations – ceaseless task.

On 30 March, Monet described a rather odd phenomenon that in his own words sounds almost like an eclipse, adding a nearly surrealistic dimension to his campaign in front of the cathedral. "Here from 2pm on, the weather turned cloudy without my realizing it, and suddenly I no longer saw the sun. Even though I waited, I was forced to take a rest. This evening, though, the sky is superb." This description corresponds to a recognizably typical weather pattern in Normandy. The sky, without any warning, may become murky and cloudy in no time and then revert to its prime state shortly thereafter.

The impression is that the light is filtered through the clouds intermittently and projected directly onto the earth.

In the same letter, mention is made of the few canvases recently started, for which he needs an extra two or three days of fine weather in order to "save" them. Despite his obsession with going home, the next day Monet considered that he might waste time unnecessarily by going back to Giverny just for the weekend, as an absence from work "is always regrettable". Nevertheless, he did spend the weekend at Giverny with Alice and returned to Rouen on Monday 3 April. He was fortunate with the weather but, as he put it, "The weather has stayed the same, but alas, it is now myself and my nerves that keep changing with each break in my work." This sentence alone reveals a very important aspect inherent to the process of creating the *Cathedrals*: the series made demands on Monet's subjectivity as well as on the objectivity of his observations. This is an aspect of Monet's work that G.H. Hamilton has amply emphasized: "We sense the difficulty he encountered in transforming the picture as a representation of something seen into a painting as an expressive work of art, that is to say, as a projection of his own inner sensibility, as a fact of consciousness rather than merely of observation."[6]

So far, throughout the excerpts of correspondence that we have examined, Monet's "shimmering record of [his own] sensations, the exquisite, iridescent chart of his acute visual sensibility"[7] was somewhat absent. To go further than Hamilton's comments on Monet's sensibility, it is true that his "*nerfs*", as Monet himself put it, or his "guts" as we might now interpret it, had a lot to do with the *Cathedrals*. Norman Rosenthal, in front of a painting from the *Cathedral* series on exhibition in Boston, put it bluntly by saying: "The weather is all in his head." However often the lighting may change, what prompts Monet to see in his paintings a "stubborn encrusting of colours" (4 April 1893) is not a simple matter-of-fact type of observation. It has to do with his own psyche. His obsessive anxiety about failure is as important a component in the making of the *Cathedral* series as is the colour of the sky or the colour of the stone: "I am greatly afraid that this will be pointless. What fate pursues me to force me to work furiously on research which is beyond my strengths."

The last few days were a complete standstill. Monet had obviously worked too hard already to perceive any change on his canvases as he added to them, and the energy he continued to expend on these works made him feel all the more frustrated. Although he worked on through his last week in Rouen it was, by his own admission, in order not to feel guilty. His last letters echoed those written at the end of his 1892 stay, reflecting depression, lack of confidence, and near desperation. Monet was angry with himself, his own "impotence" and his own weakness. He concluded that if he managed to do anything decent, it would be the result of pure chance. Monet felt that the more he persisted, the more he risked spoiling what he had achieved. "It is high time to go", he wrote on 7 April. On 11 April, he began to pack to return home. On the morning of 13 April 1893, Monet took the train back to Giverny, having asked his wife to come and meet him with two cars. Monet's study in front of the cathedral of Rouen had come to an end.

MOTIF AND SERIES

For the first and only time in his career, Monet chose to abandon his preference for a motif from nature in favour of an in-depth study of a work of art – a Gothic monument, a cultural and religious artefact. Unlike Degas, Cézanne, Renoir, or even Pissarro, Monet rarely expressed much interest in the forms of artistic tradition that had preceded Impressionism. Why, then would he abruptly decide to distance himself from nature and grapple with this monumental cultural object – the cathedral at Rouen?

The simplest answer is to dismiss the problem with a purely practical explanation. While completing recent serial works with a motif chosen from nature, Monet had experienced considerable problems. Working on a winter landscape view, for example, he was disrupted by the sudden unfurling of the trees' new leaves, as spring arrived with unexpected rapidity. Monet took the drastic step of employing someone to pick off every single leaf, so that he could pursue his painting to its pictorial conclusion despite the natural evolution of the motif itself. Similarly, when painting his *Poplars* series on the river Epte near his home at Giverny, Monet was forced to buy the trees at auction to prevent them from being cut down for matchwood before he could complete his paintings.

No doubt when settling down in front of Rouen Cathedral, Monet could be confident that no such problems would arise. The cathedral would not change its character overnight, nor would it be removed. This explanation has an irrefutable logic, but the requirement for stability and permanence would have been served equally well by any other architectural unit. It does not account for the specific choice of the Gothic cathedral as the motif for Monet's series.

The question of the motif receives only one rather disappointing answer in Monet's own words: "The motif for me is nothing but an insignificant matter – what I want to reproduce is what there is between the motif and myself."

Monet's statement simply and irrevocably discards the problem of the subject matter, since the subject that he chose to paint is "insignificant". Why try to understand why he painted a Gothic cathedral rather than anything else since, by his own admission, the visual interest to the painter lay in the air around the cathedral, saturated with light and humidity. Accepting the statement on its own terms, the particular progression of the cathedral series requires examination in the context of the immediate relationship of the painter to his motif, the fact that the series repeats the motif so insistently and precisely in thirty separate and different images, and the implications of the *Cathedral* series with regard to contemporary expectations of the painted image. However, the significance of Rouen Cathedral as a monument of Gothic art cannot be readily dismissed. The important correlations between Monet's choice of the cathedral as the motif for his series and the specific relevance of the cathedral as a work of art in its own right are discussed in detail in the following chapter.

Monet painted the air, the so-called *enveloppe* – an invisible amalgamation of air, light, moisture and temperature that alters our perception of what we see. What usually we do not see (what Monet calls the *enveloppe*) colours and transforms the visible. The reality, the subject matter in itself – the cathedral – is therefore not as important as what is around it – the invisible *enveloppe* that makes the cathedral more or less visible, that confers upon it its hues and shades, that sharpens or blurs its edges, that enhances or erases its crevices, that brings out or flattens its reliefs. For Monet, reality is not a simple, singular, monolithic concept. Monet's pictorial conception of reality, as seen through the cycle of the *Cathedrals*, establishes a fundamental distinction between the visible – the motif – and the invisible – "what there is between the motif and myself".

This distinction takes Monet's paintings far beyond the allegedly objective conception of reality generally carried out by Salon art at that time. This explains in part the problems that Monet experienced when confronted by the heralds of official art, who defended an art in which reality was globally apprehended and rendered as a whole, whose chief task was to produce an image of reality as an undivided unit unreservedly graspable by the viewers.

Besides establishing a distinction between visible and invisible, Monet founded a hierarchy between the two: the invisible commands the visible. The invisible – "what there is between the motif and myself" – is the real subject. What Monet wanted to reproduce is the distance between the cathedral and his own eyes. It could be said that Monet did not, in fact, paint the cathedral. He painted this invisible mass of air between himself and the cathedral, composed of innumerable waves of sunlight, intertwined with mist and cold, that make the cathedral visible.

The *enveloppe* filters Monet's vision of the cathedral. It colours the walls and thickens the presence of the monument; it makes the pale, neutral stone of the cathedral shine with dazzling brightness, from near-white to golden yellow, or freeze in an ethereal solid merging with the cobalt blue sky.

A practical perception of the relationship between Monet and his motif is to imagine a triangle ABC, in which each letter represents one of the three factors involved in the making of the *Cathedral* series. A represents Monet's eye in front of his canvas while he paints the cathedral. C is the cathedral itself, the visible motif. B is "what there is between the motif and myself", the *enveloppe* – or what Monet claims is his real interest and to which he attributes the greater significance in his paintings of the cathedral.

Within this triangular relationship, one can clearly discern two possible ways to go from A to C (to view the cathedral). Either A grasps C directly, or A goes via B in order to reach C. The first is the "objective", direct, traditional, immediate way to view the cathedral. This is Rouen Cathedral as Gerôme would have painted it, or as we see it reproduced in guidebooks. The relationship A-C symbolizes the way a postcard photographer or tourist would look at the cathedral: a snapshot can serve as the visual record and the eye can move on.

This simple approach cannot be of interest to Monet. He is solely interested in the triangular, complex and unbreakable relationship where C can only be apprehended through B; where B, constantly changing, constantly changes how one views C.

As will be seen in a later chapter, this rather complex way of approaching reality partly explains the huge *succès d'estime* that Monet's *Cathedrals* have enjoyed with twentieth-century artists. We have already seen that in this triangular relationship, the three elements do not carry equal function: B is clearly dominant and from its position dictates how A reaches C. Yet it is A that establishes the priority, or hierarchy, of B and C and according to Monet's own words, C is insignificant. In plate 25, for instance, the cathedral is almost totally absorbed by its *enveloppe*: its contour, its presence almost completely dissolves into the mist; the invisible has almost completely taken over the visible.

This leads to a better understanding of why Monet felt inclined to discard at once the question of his subject matter. Asked why he chose C as a motif, Monet would answer that no matter what C was,

he would paint B, an unknown and variable quantity that through its own variations necessarily transforms the relationship between A and C – the artist's eye and the motif.

For the sole purpose of demonstrating the intervention of the *enveloppe* between the artist's eye and the motif, one canvas of the individual motif would have sufficed. Monet could have decided on an interesting day to paint the cathedral once and for all, under a propitious atmospheric effect. Once the painting was achieved, the distinction between the two components of reality – the visible and the invisible – would have been clearly depicted and the trick would have been done.

By carrying through a series of works, however, Monet presents a yet more complex description of this interaction. In the thirty canvases of the *Cathedral* series, each moment and each vision of the cathedral reveals a different operation of the invisible components of the *enveloppe* on the texture of the cathedral walls. Each of these complex instants contributes to the equally complex operation of the series, of a different canvas painted to record each momentary impression. Through the device of the series, Monet's eye and hand can meticulously and painstakingly coordinate the interaction of the visible and invisible through time.

The thirty paintings can be described as a reading of the passage of time and its mark that can be almost arithmetically measured through the progression of light against shade in the morning, or of shade against light in the afternoon. Monet's paintings of the cathedral, more so than any other of his series paintings, offer a precise rendering of the effect of time on the object depicted.

In theory, as Clemenceau pointed out, each second offered a different light effect. In practice, Monet came to an unavoidable compromise. As can be reckoned from his letters from Rouen, on a good day Monet worked on nine to eleven canvases. His working day, like that of an office clerk, would last from 8am to 4 or 5pm, with one hour for lunch. Then, in spring, his evening works would take him from 4 or 5pm to 6 or 6:30pm. One can reckon that each of Monet's paintings of the cathedral represents a slice of time of 90 to 120 minutes, although in some cases the line of shadow progressing across the façade from one painting to another indicates that the span of time between two paintings can sometimes be reduced to as little as 15 to 30 minutes.

Monet's paintings of the cathedral are about time. They depict the mad race of hours, minutes, seconds – through light. In this way Monet's paintings of the cathedral take a radical stance against historical painting – a genre widely cultivated by Monet's chief opponents within the French Academy and Salon circles. Monet's *Cathedral* series can be seen as an exact reversal of a statement made by Charles Lebrun (1619–90) to members of the Académie with regard to Poussin's painting of the *Manna*: "The historical painter has only to represent one moment where simultaneous actions take place."[1]

Monet not only completely banished any narrative intention from his series, he reduced each painting to the representation of one particular slice of time – to the exclusion of what happened before or after. In an article in which he explores the iconic structure of time, Louis Marin explains that "the historical painting is a painting whose 'tense' is present, whose time is the present moment when it is seen, and the only possible way of making the story understood by the viewer, or 'read', is to distribute, all around his central represented moment, various circumstances that are logically connected to it by implication or presupposition (...) In the present presence of the pictorial representation [the historical painting], it has to express diachrony, temporal relationships, yet can do so only through the network of a whole that generates its parts logically or achronically by its own signifying economy. The time of the story, its succeeding parts related to the succession of events, is neutralized in the intelligible space of a model that represents only the logical relationships of elements subordinated to a centre."[2]

No such paradox can be found in Monet's paintings of the cathedral. Each painting is the immediate vision of an "effect" that took place "instantaneously" on the cathedral façade, in front of Monet's eyes. To catch the effect of a few minutes, of a given hour, indicated by the position of the light on the wall, is one essential point of each painting of the cathedral. While historical and "realistic" painting in the nineteenth-century French Academy produced paintings that appeared a-chronical, a-temporal (timeless), because the artist tried to cram too many time sequences into a single canvas, Monet proposed a radical break with this type of art, by reinjecting one sequence of time at a time within one particular canvas.

It may not be sheer coincidence that almost every painting of the cathedral centres on the clock; a clock that, ironically a victim of the vicissitudes of time, eventually fell off the wall and is no longer visible. The "before" and the "after", the "not yet" and the "already gone" are not to be found in a single painting of the cathedral by Monet. Each painting is depicting the "right now", the hour that is marked on the clock – which, however, Monet chose to blur with paint. The clock reveals only a crust of colours. Monet divorces each sequence of time from another in the series. No such thing as the guarantee of a permanent truth is to be found: each painting is the truth of an instant, negated by the one before, and the one after.

The series dismisses the idea of a permanent reality for which a faithful pictorial sign could be substituted. But, paradox of paradoxes, to make this experiment in instantaneous vision, Monet chooses to paint a cathedral whose secular existence guarantees a certain permanence. And, lastly, it took him years to achieve, in pictorial terms, the visual effects of a series of instants. In effect, then, Monet clearly dissociated the time of the eye from the time of the hand – dwelling on the huge divide between the time of viewing and the time of painting – instead of amalgamating them through various illusory devices, as in the case of history painting. Monet, arch-typically in the case of the *Cathedrals*, distinguishes and complexifies the two forms of time inherent to creation. By so doing, Monet conferred an autonomy on the time of creating (of "making", what one might call the time of *poiesis*) which was to find some notable echoes in contemporaneous poetry: with Mallarmé and Valéry, for instance, for whom "the line evolved toward autonomy, escaping the meaning that it holds".

As Valéry wrote: "My lines have had no other interest, for myself, than to raise thoughts about the poet." Paraphrasing Valéry, one might say that the whole point of Monet's *Cathedrals* is to raise thoughts about the painter. In both cases the work (painting or poem) opens itself onto the movement and the timing that makes it possible. Monet's *Cathedrals* tell us the story of the wide and infinite search for their own sources. Monet, for this purpose, chose to paint the cathedral which itself is rooted in the tension between temporality and intemporality, between human or worldly time and divine time, that is, eternity.

THE SIGNIFICANCE OF THE GOTHIC

"It must not be forgotten that the Gothic artists were inventors and that we may have to perform, not better, which is impossible, but differently and following our own bent. The results will not be immediately evident."

CAMILLE PISSARRO, LETTER TO HIS SON
ROUEN, 19 AUGUST 1898

Even if we accept Monet's own statement that the motif is an insignificant matter, we might still ask why the artist did not choose an insignificant object. Why not have chosen a belfry or a nineteenth-century town hall or, as a critic among Monet's contemporaries proposed, a cube of stone? Whatever Monet's insistence on the insignificance of his motif, the Gothic cathedral at Rouen is not insignificant as an object. In fact, one of the paradoxes inherent to this series and particularly worthy of attention is the extraordinary significance of the cathedral.

Rouen Cathedral stands, inside and outside Monet's series, as a marvellous monument of Gothic architecture. The cathedral can precisely be called marvellous in the sense that Gregory of Tours, in the sixth century, attributed to various marvels, endowed with a biblical connotation, that were "works of men but of men implicitly or explicitly acting under divine inspiration or guidance".[1] It also stands association with a text by an anonymous author of the twelfth century describing these same marvels, "which age will not render old, accidents cannot destroy, time cannot diminish, and whose end cannot precede the end of all things."[2]

It is not at all incompatible to seek what the builders of the cathedral of Rouen were aiming at, at the same time as considering Monet's series of paintings of the cathedral. While Monet dismissed the pre-eminence of the subject matter over the *enveloppe* and never entered the finer discussion of why any given subject might be more appropriate than another to his pictorial activity, the fact remains that when he set his mind on painting a cathedral he selected a work of art, a monument of Gothic architecture, as his motif – or, to be more precise, as a background to his study of the *enveloppe* of light surrounding the cathedral.

Monet, unlike most of his fellow Impressionists, showed remarkably little interest in the art of the past. His correspondence of the 1890s almost never carries any reference to earlier artists. In fact, during that period, he seemed even to withdraw from communication with his contemporaries. His only two regular correspondents were Alice Hoschedé, who became his wife in 1892, and his dealer Durand-Ruel: there were rare letters to a few colleagues such as Helleu, Whistler, Pissarro, Zola and Mallarmé. On a painting expedition to the South of France, a few years before starting the *Cathedral* series, Monet was careful to avoid the company of Renoir. Like the career of a scientist or saint, Monet's pictorial development at this time appears singularly isolated. From start to end, Monet was very much on his own, apparently impervious to influences from the past or the present. With the exception of Boudin, Monet did not acknowledge a debt to any other artist.

In a beautiful and very evocative text written *c.* 1854, when Monet was still only in his twenties, Boudin unwittingly described the role that was to be undertaken by Monet: "Sometimes during my melancholy walks, I gaze on this light that inundates the earth, that quivers on the water, that plays on clothing, and I grow faint to realize how much genius is needed to master so many difficulties, how limited is the power of man's mind to put all these things together in his brain. Then I feel that poetry is there."[3]

Realizing how little time was available to him and how limited was the power of his mind to master the near-titanic pictorial tasks that he had set himself, Monet never had time for anything else, or anyone else. His letters to Alice show that he was frequently prepared to give his work precedence over his family and his home. Monet's individualistic and self-sufficient painterly pursuits completely defuse the traditional tools and devices of the art historian in search of "revealing influences". In this context, it appears all the more conspicuous that Monet's almost unique interest in any form of art other than his own was focused upon a Gothic cathedral. Whether Monet was aware of it or not, this interest found an echo in the concerns of two of his colleagues.

Renoir found in Gothic architecture a perfect stance against contemporary architecture for which he professed the greatest dislike. Renoir was quite strongly opinionated in his views on modern architecture and voiced his conceptions in a treatise that was never published, called *Grammaire à l'usage de jeunes architectes*.[4] Here he made specific reference to Rouen Cathedral, as opposed to the ugliness of nineteenth-century buildings: "One gets used to it; one no longer sees that it is ugly. When we became totally accustomed to it, that will be the end of a civilization that gave us the Parthenon and Rouen Cathedral. Men will be committing suicide out of boredom and killing themselves for pleasure."

One cannot help smiling at the somewhat naive classification that cites the Parthenon and Rouen Cathedral as the two noteworthy landmarks of a civilization whose values are decaying. Equally interesting is Renoir's apocalyptic and lugubrious vision of what will be the human result of this decay.

For Renoir, without any doubt, "the modern architect is, in general, the greatest enemy of art."[5] However, the solution that he suggests to young architects is definitely not to copy medieval architecture: "there are people who believe that one can do the Middle Ages without strain . . . we only know how to copy, this is our Shibboleth. And when this little ceremony has lasted long enough, just go and look at the source. You will see how far away we are!!"[6]

What Renoir retains among all great architecture is the fact that *"les grands maîtres"*, as he calls them, "created irregularity in regularity". When looking at the landmarks of past civilization, at the centre of which Renoir places Rouen Cathedral, he noted, as a characteristic, that all the buildings were perfectly regular as a whole, although no one is identical to another.

It is impossible to establish whether Monet had any knowledge of Renoir's treatise, or whether he knew of Renoir's feelings on the subject. In the overall regularity of the outer structure of the cathedral offset by the amazing irregularity of the details on the façade, Monet found fertile ground for his experimentation with light. Monet summarized this contrast in a condensed sentence with a somewhat poetical and almost Mallarméan ring: "Everything changes, even stone."[7]

A definite taste for the Gothic among the Impressionists is represented in these architectural considerations by Renoir. References to Gothic art are also found in abundance in Pissarro's correspondence, where the artist frequently expresses his fervour for an epoch that was somewhat overlooked by the contemporaries of the Impressionists.

In a letter to his son Lucien, sent from Rouen on 20 November 1883, Pissarro wrote: "I have also made some drawings from wood sculptures, pure Gothic, with a few ornaments, they are simply marvellous. This is how one realizes what the realism of that period was."[8] Later on, offering artistic advice to Lucien, Pissarro wrote:

"Don't forget (. . .) Gothic figures, the real ones like those we saw in Rouen."[9]

In another very enthusiastic letter describing the marvels of the Gothic Rouen that Pissarro discovered, he vividly took up the defence of Rouen against those who failed to see in the city anything but banality and triviality: "Really! That imbecile Mourey is a brute to believe that it is banal and trivial. It is as beautiful as Venice, my dear, it has extraordinary character and really it is beautiful! (. . .) There are wonders at right and left . . ."[10]

In another fascinating letter, Pissarro reveals a certain allegiance to Gothic art: "If I must suffer an influence, I would prefer to suffer that of the real Gothics that I have at every instant in my sight here. It is stunning how they capture nature, being at the same time very decorative, without the preciousness and sentimentality of those modern painters who call themselves their students"[11] Pissarro here echoes Renoir's warning against trying to "copy" Gothic art too faithfully, by criticizing those who call themselves the "pupils" of Gothic art.

Renoir, Pissarro and Monet, all in different and individual ways, experienced a strong and sustained fascination for Gothic art. What is apparent through these texts is that both Renoir and Pissarro mistrust the tendency to imitate the Gothic through copying. Although Pissarro himself repeatedly advocates copying Gothic works to his son Lucien, there is little evidence that he or his son actually did so. One exception in Pissarro's work is a study of a carved figure, executed in 1883, whose rarity was thus underscored by Richard Brettell and Christopher Lloyd: "In spite of Pissarro's constant advice to his son Lucien to copy other works of art, especially sculpture [this drawing] is Camille Pissarro's only surviving drawing after an original piece of sculpture. Indeed, it is one of his very rare direct copies after a work of art."[12]

This leads us here to establish a fine distinction with regard to Monet's *Cathedral* series. Monet's paintings of Rouen Cathedral clearly are not copies of a work of art, and the canvases do not reproduce the fine detail of the sculptures on the cathedral façade. Yet the paintings constitute a singular example in Monet's career of a work of art about another work of art.

When Pissarro refers so admiringly to Gothic art, particularly in Rouen, he often emphasizes its high degree of realism. A few questions that can be raised in respect to that Gothic "realism" definitely shed a different light on Monet's paintings of Rouen Cathedral.

The cathedral at Rouen, like all Gothic cathedrals, embodied a certain conception of reality. What, exactly, was the vision of things that presided over the construction of Rouen Cathedral? What did the Gothic architects who built Monet's subject try to say, and how did they try to say it? These are questions that should necessarily colour our ways of looking at Monet's *Cathedrals*. In painting thirty canvases that are about the cathedral, Monet represented a mode of representation of reality. Rouen Cathedral itself portrays reality in a certain mode. The assumption made here is not that a causal or deterministic link exists between the Gothic cathedrals and Monet's paintings of Rouen Cathedral. In other words, the point is not to reveal influences of the Gothics on Monet but rather to point out several thematic correlations between Monet's series of paintings in front of Rouen Cathedral and the Gothic idiom itself and to analyse the various analogies between the mode of vision of the Gothics and that of Monet while painting the Cathedral. The result, far from leading to the statement that one dictated the other, should rather mutually enrich our perception of the art of the Gothics and of Monet.

Whether Monet was aware of it, or it all remained unconscious, or was all sheer coincidence, one cannot but observe a definite convergence of themes and a community of concerns between Monet's pictorial stance and some tenets of Gothic architecture. As Emile Mâle wrote in his voluminous opus on Gothic art published only four years after Monet's *Cathedral* series was completed, Gothic art, through a complex grid of symbols, allowed the artist "to express the invisible" and "to represent what is beyond the domain of art".[13]

Likewise, in this context, a definition of Gothic architecture given by Otto von Simson provides a relevant association to Monet's *Cathedrals*. Simson understands Gothic architecture as "an image, more precisely, as the representation of supernatural reality".[14] Gothic architecture looks beyond nature – to see in it the mark, the symbol of God's creation. Monet, in his paintings of the cathedral, examines those aspects of the reality of his subject – the effects of light, the weight of the atmosphere and the transformations made by the weather – usually unsuspected and left unremarked. For both the Gothic architect and the Impressionist painter, reality only stands as a pretext to express something else – something invisible. In the former case, it is the principles of creation – God and his word; in the latter, it is what makes reality visible, while itself remaining invisible – the air or the *enveloppe*, an invisible filter of light.

The kinship that immediately strikes us between the principles that informed Gothic architecture and the stimulus that informed Monet's *Cathedral* series is basically a profound questioning of the relevance of depicting reality *per se* as a monolithic object. Both the Impressionist artist and the Gothic architect look beyond or beneath what they see. Is what we see really what we see? is a question that can be asked with the same pertinence in relation to both the cathedral builders and the painter of the cathedral. Monet reflecting this point, admitted to Clemenceau: "While you are searching for the world in itself philosophically, . . . I simply gear my efforts on a maximum of appearances in narrow correlation with *unknown realities*, . . . when one is on the level of concordant appearances, one cannot be that far from reality – or at least from what we can know of it."[14a]

Both the Gothics and Monet established a strong and compelling dialectic between reality and appearance that can leave us perplexed. What we consider obvious is in fact not so obvious. Monet, painting in front of the cathedral, did not paint the cathedral. In his own words, he painted what was between the cathedral and himself: the in-between, the distance. The cathedral in Monet's paintings is therefore veiled by the invisible – by the air, and by the light that surreptitiously transforms what we see, and yet was never before Monet a subject of interest.

"Is the world only appearance? Does it have reality?"[15] It is interesting to see how Emile Mâle answered these two questions from the Gothic standpoint, and how the questions and answers can be seen equally to relate to Monet's vision of the cathedral. "In the Middle Ages, the response would have been unanimous: the world is a symbol. The universe is a thought which God carried within himself in the beginning, as an artist carries in his soul the idea of his work. God created, but he created through his Word, or through his Son. It was the Son who accomplished the thought of the Father, who transformed potentiality into act. The Son is the real creator. Imbued with this doctrine, medieval artists always represented the Creator in the person of Christ (. . .) According to the theologians, God the Father created *in principio*, that is *in verbo*, through his Word, his Son. Jesus was the author both of Creation and of Redemption."[16] "Thus the world can be defined in this way: 'An idea of God realized by the Word'. If such be the case, each being conceals a divine thought."[17]

The intention here is certainly not to force on Monet's *Cathedral* series a grid of religious symbols that he most likely would have ignored. What seems important, in this context, in order to perceive more precisely the principal root of Monet's approach to the *Cathedral* series, is to recognize that the Gothics did not take visible, tangible

reality for granted. Neither did Monet. In that sense, Gothic architecture offers an ideal precedent for Monet's challenge to those who, in the nineteenth century, felt that a painter absolutely "must know how to reproduce with exact truth the appearance of every feature of a site."[18]

For Monet, nature never could be grasped as a whole; trees, rivers, fields and sky could never be reproduced faithfully all at once, since "nature", together with its *enveloppe*, was in a constant tremor; since the light that made it more or less visible was itself in continual change; since the whole of reality was in perpetual movement. By deciding upon painting the cathedral, Monet took his stance one step further, by demonstrating that even the façade of a Gothic church, permanent, static and solid as it may be, or appear to be, does not resist the changes imposed by light. Light in its intangible, immaterial, invisible essence, embraces even the solid, massive, impermeable stone structure of a cathedral and transforms it from day to day, from hour to hour, so that the cathedral will perennially appear to differ from itself.

It is interesting that Monet chose to depict Rouen Cathedral for this experiment, since the cathedral itself embodied a major split between what we might broadly call the visible and the invisible. Of course, this characteristic split conveys two radically different functions according to whether it is examined in the context of Gothic art or of Monet's *Cathedral* series. The split between the visible and the invisible is metaphysical for the Gothics: it is quintessentially physical in Monet's case.

For the Gothic, there was the real and there was the Divine. The cathedral addressed this issue by having one (the real) signify and refer symbolically to the other (the Divine). In Monet's case, there is no reference whatsoever to the divine, or to an upper, immaterial world. The split in Monet's cathedral is a physical one – between light and stone. Both realities, in each case, are necessary to each other, and cannot be conceived without each other.

In Gothic art, the real is wholly dependent on God's act of creation. The animals, plants, rivers and oceans depicted on the stone façade of the cathedrals call symbolically for their author. The split in Gothic art is metaphysical and moral, reflecting the division of the two worlds conceived by Saint Augustine – the upper world (the Divine) and the lower world (the human, mundane one). This establishes a hierarchy, a system of moral values. The split in Gothic art is therefore a vertical one, between here and above.

The split in Monet's paintings of Rouen Cathedral is horizontal: it is to be found "between the motif and myself". It is the difference between the cathedral itself and the light, air, wind, fog, sunshine, and the passage of time, that intervene between the painter and his subject. No moral hierarchy is to be derived from this difference.

In fact, the comparison with Gothic art is here again very telling. In the Gothic conception, the difference between the two worlds, the upper and lower, transcends mankind. In Monet's conception, the difference between the motif and "what there is between the motif and myself" is inherent to humanity. This fact, this division, is really the subject matter of Monet's series of the cathedral. The plastic conceptions of Gothic art and Monet's pictorial conceptions both depend upon refuting a monolithic vision that faithfully depicts a unified, wholesome, coherent reality.

However, a large difference is to be stressed between the conceptual foundation of a Gothic cathedral and Monet's principle in painting the *Cathedral* series. We have seen that the distinction is of a metaphysical nature in terms of the Gothic, and a physical one in Monet's case. Translated in terms of time, the difference contained within the Gothic concept becomes one between eternity – the upper, invisible world – and mortal life – the lower, visible world. Whereas in Monet's paintings, the split is inherent to each second:

each instant carries a different effect of the contact between light, air, mist, warmth or cold, and the actual structure of the cathedral.

Thus, for Monet, the division between the invisible and the visible is not chronological, in the sense that it is not a matter of eternity succeeding mortal life; it is inherent to our vision. The confrontation between the air and light (invisible) and stone (visible) is continually recurrent and inherent to our vision or, at least, certainly to Monet's vision. The two are constantly in contact, constantly interfering with each other. As we can see in many of the cathedral paintings, the sky or air sometimes seems to be piercing through the stone – the air seems to become stone, while the stone itself is vaporizing. Monet is painting the contact, the shock, the interferences of these elements.

Monet and the Gothics both introduce an ethereal element into the configuration of their works. In the construction of the cathedral it is referred to as a transcendant principle, Heaven, of which the cathedral is merely an earthly shadow. In the making of Monet's *Cathedral* series, the ethereal is present everywhere, surrounding the cathedral with its all-encompassing *enveloppe*, filling the intervals, reflecting, vibrating against the stone façade, shaping or unshaping the details of the sculpture and architecture. It is not referred to symbolically, as in the original construction of the cathedral, it is depicted as an imminent force, painted as an element perspiring through the stone, imbuing the cathedral with all its presence. The sky becomes part of the cathedral, struggling with or caressing the stone façade.

Both conceptions transcend the norms of imagery. Both attitudes reject the notion of a single uniform reality that prevailed in nineteenth-century academic painting. However, Monet brings the invisible within the realms of the visible – light and air become concrete reality and can be apprehended visually and poetically. In Gothic architecture, the role of the invisible is deferred to the realm of God – active though absent, real though distant.

A compelling aspect of Gothic art that must be brought in to form a more complete backdrop to Monet's *Cathedral* series is the Gothic concept of light. One of the most fundamental deciding factors of Gothic art is precisely the use of light, and not, as we often believe, the recourse to cross-ribbed vaults, pointed arches or flying buttresses. These, as Otto von Simson points out, are "constructive means but not artistic ends."[19] The Gothics were most innovative insofar as their architecture was inherently expressing "the relation of light to the material substance of the walls".[20] This particular concept is perhaps the most concise and essential definition that could equally be given for Monet's *Cathedral* series.

Simson depicts in a few words the implications of this definition of Gothic art: "The Gothic wall seems to be porous: light filters through it, permeating it, merging with it, transfiguring it."[21] Simson sees in the stained-glass windows not just "openings in the walls" to admit light, but "transparent walls". "As Gothic verticalism seems to reverse the movement of gravity, so by a similar aesthetic paradox, the stained-glass window seemingly denies the impenetrable nature of matter, receiving its visual existence from an energy that transcends it. Light, which is ordinarily concealed by matter, appears as the active principle; and matter is aesthetically real only insofar as it partakes of and is defined by the luminous quality of light." He further explains that the exterior walls of the cathedral "pierced by continuous rows of windows" ultimately appear as "a shallow transparent shell" around the nave, while the windows "seem to merge, vertically and horizontally, into a continuous sphere of light, a luminous foil behind all tactile forms of the architectural system."[22]

The visual and aesthetic concerns thus described are clearly analogous to those of Monet in his *Cathedral* series. In both the Gothic construction of a cathedral and in the impressionistic depiction of Rouen Cathedral, the pattern of the architectural structure is "dramatically articulated by light", through the stone's fragile structure, in the former case, and through paint, in the latter.

Naturally, we recognize here that the use of light intricately playing against the skeleton of stone carries out a totally different function in the construction of the cathedrals from that in Monet's paintings of Rouen Cathedral. The signification of light in the medieval conception of the world is here to be referred, as in everything, to its theological function.[23] In fact, the primary recourse to light by the Gothic builders, who gave to it as much weight and importance as to stone, was nothing like a decorative or ornamental fancy on the part of the architects. The reason why it was so vital to elevate the stone with light in the making of those cathedrals was the concept of God as light.

In the theological system recorded in the text known as *Theologia Mystica*, which was absolutely central to the conception of the cathedrals, God is presented as the initial light, uncreated, the source of all creatures. Each creature receives a certain degree of illumination according to its place in the universal hierarchy created by God. The universe itself is a vast luminous splash, comparable to a fountain of light that would fall in cascades and irrigate the world down to the lowest level of creation. Every creature unveils, to the extent that it can, the splendour of God.

What transpires in this conception and sheds a new light, as it were, on Monet's own *Cathedrals*, is that we find here an essentially relativist approach to the perception and the rendering of light. The point being, in the context of the *Cathedral* series, that it would be thought as totally impossible for the painter to render the cathedral in "perfect", "ideal" or "objective" light as it would have been for a Gothic architect to render the absolute source of light – God, invisible by essence, incomprehensible by nature.

A s much as the structures of the Gothic building were apt to convey, aesthetically and theologically, the divine irradiation that was reflected in the fusion of light and stone, various objects were also thought of as inherently appropriate to reflect the divine iridescence – and therefore to convey, symbolically, the radiance of truth. We find here another parallel between Monet and medieval theologians. Gems are used, by both Monet and the Gothics namely, to illustrate the fusion between light and stone. Indeed, like stones that have become porous to light, translucent coloured gemstones filter light and in them light turns into a solid element. The medieval theologians gave to gems a singular, moral value: they were one significant symbol that could lead the soul to progress from the created (stone) to the uncreated (light), from the material to the immaterial. For Monet, gems were a useful image, a lexical and poetical equivalent for his pictorial concerns.

We find an early link between the symbolic function of gems in the medieval imagination and the actuality of Gothic architecture in the laying of the foundation stone for the choir of the Abbey of Saint-Denis. As Louis VII, King of France, was performing this solemn duty, he was given a handful of gems, which he laid next to the foundation stones. In the background, the clerics and monks were singing the psalm "Thy walls are precious stones".[24] The sparkling glitter of the gems contributed to the shower of light converging on the choir where the divine office took place. The Abbot Suger, architect of the Basilica of Saint-Denis, explained that fascination for gems: "As I am completely absorbed by the enchantment of the beauty of the house of God, the charm of the multi-coloured gems has led me, while transposing that which is material into that which is immaterial, to reflect on the diversity of sacred virtues; then it appears to me that I see myself dwelling as in reality in some strange region of the universe, which existed previously neither in the mud of the earth nor in the purity of the sun, and that by the grace of God, I can be transported from down here into the higher world in an anagogical manner."[25]

There are two particularly resonant references to precious stones among Monet's letters, in both cases introduced to explain what he sees and tries to render in paint. The first is in a letter to Rodin written on 1 February 1888 from Antibes: "I am fencing and struggling with the sun – and what a sun here! We ought to paint here with gold and precious stones. It is admirable."[26]

In a letter written to Alice Hoschedé on 3 May 1889 from the Creuse valley, Monet expresses his amazement at "so many changes, and the sun reflecting in the water into splinters of diamond. I almost gave up, since it is dazzling."[27]

The latter reference is more restrained, more comparative and less daring than the former. The metaphor that Monet resorted to in his letter to Rodin is astonishingly poetic, vividly evoking Monet's sense that oil paint has become inadequate to rendering the effects of the powerful meridian light, and that the appropriate media for his work would be those that could contain or transmit light – gold and gems.

The poetical impact of Monet's expression in his letter to Rodin is certainly as fortuitous and as strong as the symbolic gesture of King Louis VII laying the handful of gems with the first stone of the Basilica of Saint-Denis in the twelfth century.

What clearly derives from this comparative analysis is, however, that although the conceptions presiding over Gothic architecture and Monet's paintings differ radically, the materials that kindled the imaginations of the Gothic architects and of the Impressionist painter are remarkably analogous. It is apparent that for both, "light was the source and essence of all visual beauty".[28] The theme of the fusion and the contrast of light and stone had the same emotive connotation, the same affective potency, in the erecting of the cathedrals as in the painting of one of these cathedrals by Monet six hundred years later. It is a theme that resorts essentially to poetry insofar as it breaks up the codes of conventional understanding. Light, in reality, does not go through stone, only in Monet's imagination and in the minds of the medieval theologians who presided over the conception of the cathedral. Each sees in this imaginary theme totally different semantic contents; both, however, resort to it plastically.

These two forms of plastic creation – architectural and pictorial – apparently lead to diametrically opposed "conclusions". The Gothics used the intricacies of the intermingling of light and stone as a means to reveal (or suggest) the invisible but ever-present existence of God. Monet, on the other hand, studied and exploited the same theme pictorially for its own sake, making it a purely impressionistic, purely atheistic or agnostic issue.

A proper understanding of the role of light in both the cathedral architecture and in Monet's paintings must include the question of the cathedral's orientation. As we know, all but two of the paintings that constitute the series depict the western façade of Rouen Cathedral. We may wonder why he particularly chose to focus on this aspect. The question receives a very interesting answer when put in the context of medieval theory on the orientation of a church. As Emile Mâle explained in his study, "a strictly respected rule had established that churches and cathedrals were to be oriented from east to west".[29] For the Gothic architects, the course of the sun was a vital factor in locating the foundations of a church. From the

eleventh to the sixteenth centuries, almost no exception can be found to this rule, although it would be wrong to assume that this consideration was inherent to the construction of all churches, as the rule gradually became forgotten after the Gothic era and by the mid-sixteenth century was no longer respected.

Each cardinal point had its own significance.[30] The east pointed toward Jerusalem, the Heavenly City, and indicated the renewal of light. The north, the "region of cold and night, was usually devoted to the Old Testament".[31] The south, "warmed by the sun and bathed in full light was devoted to the New Testament." The west façade carried the representation of the Last Judgement. The explanation for this was that "the setting sun illuminated this great scene of the last evening of the world".[32]

Description in the Book of Revelation inspired the complex profusion of carved imagery found on the western fronts of almost all of the Gothic cathedrals. "And he who sat there appeared like jasper and carnelian, and round the throne was a rainbow that looked like an emerald, round the throne were twenty-four thrones, and seated on the thrones were twenty-four elders, clad in white garments, with golden crowns upon their heads. From the throne issue flashes of lightning, and voices and peals of thunder, and before the throne burn seven torches of fire, which are the seven spirits of God; and before the throne there is as it were a sea of glass, like crystal. And round the throne, on each side of the throne, are four living creatures, full of eyes in front and behind."[33]

Thus the structure of the cathedral, at Rouen and elsewhere, deals with something of a supernatural vision. The Creator, set against a background of stars and surrounded by creatures dazzled by his splendour, witnesses the cataclysm of the last hour – a storm of fires and bright flashes of light, a blinding firework of lightning and thunderbolts. This scene, in order to obtain its full significance, needed the carnation of the sunset light to set ablaze the scene on the stone façade.

Monet also needed the sunlight to be crushed on the stone façade in order to reach his effects, although he totally deprived his work of any of the narrative, dramatic or religious content so crucial to the Gothic conception. In fact, it would be a useless exercise to look for any trace of a detail relating to the biblical text in Monet's paintings of Rouen Cathedral, but this would be to miss the point entirely. The point is that one can identify another certain analogy, or an equation of relationships, between Monet and his subject matter, on the one hand, and between the cathedral artists and their own subject matter. This analogy totally preserves the differences and the identities of these separate but related works of art – Monet's series and the cathedral itself. However, if dealt with in a fruitful and methodic way, the analogy helps us to address a visual and poetic continuum between the subject matter of Monet's paintings and the subject matter of their motif, that is, of Rouen Cathedral.

The western façade of the cathedral amounted to a huge challenge for the Gothic artist and, naturally, for Monet also, a few centuries later. To quote Emile Mâle again: "What sculptor would dare attempt such a scene in which 'the Heaven departed as a book folded up' . . . and what painter could reproduce the resplendent colours of the Heavenly Jerusalem – sapphire, emerald, chrysophase?"[34]

And what painter, one might have asked, could reproduce the very same façade under the resplendent colours of every changing hour?

CATHEDRALS AND CRITICS

"Certainly no photograph and least of all no words can convey the peculiar quality of the paint in these pictures."
GEORGE HEARD HAMILTON [1]
Monet: Rouen Cathedral, 1960

Claude Monet's series of Rouen Cathedral, though revolving obsessively around precisely the same architectural motif, heightens our awareness of pictorial form and of chromatic richness, as the subject matter itself dissolves into a crusty, sensitively worked surface of paint. The subjective element plays, here at least, as great a role as the objective one.

This opposition between the subjective and the objective was a central issue in the interpretation of Monet's series. Often contradictory, even occasionally polemical, many of the widely ranging responses provoked by the *Cathedral* paintings remain significant today. Most interpretations of this chromatic venture tend to dwell on one or two particular points about the paintings, and to reduce the series as a whole to those points. In the end, therefore, a reading of the critics' accounts of the *Cathedrals* reflects more upon the history of critical sensibility than upon the *Cathedral* series itself, more upon the answers supplied to the questions raised by those paintings than upon the complexity of the questions themselves.

An early account of what the *Cathedrals* looked like, written before the Durand-Ruel 1895 exhibition, offers little critical acumen: it was given by a somewhat unexpected witness, Prince Eugen of Sweden (the King of Sweden's younger son) who met Monet in Norway in 1894. Besides its anecdotal charm, this written account proves that Monet took his *Cathedrals* (or at least a few of them) with him wherever he went, and that even while doing something entirely different, he was still thinking about reworking the series.

The Prince's written observations deserve quotation: "While I listened to the master, my eyes wandered through the half-open door to the adjoining room. It was clearly Monet's just-mentioned 'meditation room'. In it I saw, among many scattered, unfinished paintings, a large canvas showing a sculptured stone façade, seen almost without perspective and distance, a visionary picture of a church façade – incredible, fascinating, fantastic as an idea. The painting was in progress. I understood that I was seeing a sample of Monet's by then nearly legendary series of Rouen Cathedral. I drew our host's attention to what I had happened to glimpse. Monet opened the door hesitantly. 'I shouldn't be showing that picture in this state,' he explained. 'I'm trying to get it into shape. It is costing me a great deal of difficulty.' When we had left and were down on the street, Thaulow remarked: 'I guess we just penetrated the holy of holies of Monet's "headquarters".' But it has some advantage to be able to steal a first peek at something. For we are without a doubt the first to have seen a Cathedral."[2]

The critical response was very clearly polarized. Two critics, both leading art writers, Gustave Geffroy and Georges Clemenceau, were unreservedly enthusiastic. Most other criticism, while offering conventional acknowledgment of Monet's talent, was generally cooler, although seldom did any critic dismiss the works outright and all were obliged to recognize the prodigious achievement and aesthetic impact of the series. Importantly, the criticism was typically based upon the individual critics' *idées fixes* concerning Monet's work, and while this body of critical writing suggested interesting areas of argument, many of these were not properly explored until considerably later.

An article written by Camille Mauclair at the time of the Durand-Ruel show[3] is very representative of the general tendency prevailing among those critics who had dismissed Impressionism in its early days and were forced eventually to recognize some of its importance. "I can almost say nothing about the capital event of this month, that is, the exhibition at Durand-Ruel's of Monsieur Claude Monet's 'Cathedrals', so eagerly awaited." This weak concession to the decisive importance of the event is followed by an elaborate compliment certainly intended as no compliment at all: "M. Monet is undeniably the most prodigious virtuoso that French painting has seen since Manet." Then, after a formal and superficial description of the content of the exhibition, Mauclair proceeds to investigate the weaknesses he sees in the series of paintings: "This series of the portals of Rouen at every hour and in every kind of light is amazing in its mastery, its strength, its bright colours, its delicacy and its magic. (…) Perhaps Monsieur Monet goes a little too far in the iridescence. Certain portals look multi-coloured and seem blended in the azure of the tropics. Others are drowning in a powdery effect that rejoices the eye, but disturbs the impression of severity of these old Gothic stones."

Within those few perplexed and awkwardly equivocal lines, Mauclair hints at some of the crucial issues of the *Cathedral* paintings. The first of Mauclair's objections is that the paintings "go too far." Monet's unbridled iridescence reminds him of a mad blue tropical sky. The excess or exaggeration Mauclair clumsily refers to in his article is a constant refrain in contemporary criticism of Monet's *Cathedral* series. It tends to suggest that Monet's palette and brush should have been more reserved and subdued – as though there were some sort of sin outlined behind the coloured surfaces of the paintings. André Michel, another art critic of the time, echoed Mauclair's criticism in even less complimentary terms: "there is no doubt here that these *Cathedrals* are in no way studies after nature, or direct or sincere observations. (…) The procedure has something exasperated and morbid. (…) After such an effort and so astonishing a challenge, such abuse and such a shattering of the profession, oil painting has no longer anything to say."[4] It should be noticed, incidentally, that both Mauclair and Michel seem to suggest that there is nothing left to say after having seen the *Cathedral* paintings. For all their supposed hyperbole, abuse and excess, the paintings force us into silence.

The critical stress on the excessive, exasperated aspect of the paintings finds a counterpoint in Monet's letters. In a letter written to Geffroy, on 28 March 1893, he clearly expressed how he saw the problem of making the *Cathedral* series finite or complete (as discussed in the Introduction). However, both Mauclair and Michel made more than a sheer plastic argument out of this lack of boundaries. Both of those critics saw in Monet's, "excess" not only an indication that the *Cathedrals* may have terminated the history of oil painting, but also a ground for moral blame. How does one distinguish, they seem to suggest, an extremely acute sensibility from indulgent sensuality? André Michel's choice of words is in this respect very significant. It is on the cathedrals that "M. Monet edifies his experiments, or rather, more precisely, he abandons himself [*assouvit*] to his ecstatic lyricism in these brilliant and arbitrary evocations."[5] "*Assouvir*" is generally used in French to suggest appeasing a violent desire, or to satisfy or to give way to a burning passion. By using these connotations, Michel seemed to imply that

Monet was under some sort of uncontrollable mental or sexual disorder. The final extension of this point, by Mauclair was that the paintings were insulting, disorderly, sensual, orgiastic and even blasphemous. Mauclair's analysis turned a technical interpretation into a moral argument: "Colour wanders with some insolence around these Middle Ages disturbed by a disorderly genius. Monet's effort is considerable and particularly significant. After a life of shimmering sensuality, to grapple with the verticality of these pictures, where all the planes are reduced to a single one, and to attempt to apply to these ascents of monochromatic stone, to these linear definitions, an art which is exclusively colour-concerned and *orgiastic*, this is the deed of a very audacious and very powerful man. The very idea that Gothic art, a quintessentially cerebral art, has provided a theme for this so superbly sensual pagan, is somewhat hurtful. (...) All that his [Monet's] genius does is to add excessive colour – admirable but excessive – to these façades, which, by the sole fact of their orientation and of their rhythm, signify plastically as much as these fireworks, and signify morally everything that they negate."[6]

This argument is founded on the following simplistic equations: colour=carnality, visual pleasure=sensuality, as opposed to Gothic art=linear structure=clear physical restraint (severity, austerity). To superimpose one on the other is synonymous with moral contradiction or blasphemy.

The association of lack of moral restraint with the *Cathedral* series was only characteristic of the puritanical fringe of critics. Although it found a strong echo with subsequent generations, it was certainly not representative of all critics of the time. The element they drew attention to was, however, to be stressed and developed more emphatically by future generations of critics was the lack of plastic definition – the absence of drawing. No delineations meant no physical or plastic limits. For Mauclair, as for Michel, Monet's *Cathedral* paintings were all about colour. The complexity and severity of the architectural motif was absorbed and dissolved in the hazy effects produced by colour alone. To Mauclair, every part of the series manifested Monet's inability to make the lines suggest anything clear. Half a century later, Clement Greenberg was to develop the same issue in a more precise and suggestive way. By then, however, the quality of the paintings was no longer an issue.

Among contemporary critics of Monet, Clemenceau and Geffroy took a radically different stance on the *Cathedrals*. Although they were the first to recognize in their own terms the spectacular quality of the series, their texts deserve renewed attention. Geffroy's text is more analytical than Clemenceau's; he paid more attention to the compositional devices involved in the making of a picture. Yet, what is of particular interest in Clemenceau's text, besides his prodigious enthusiasm for the pictures, is the almost symmetrically opposite effect they produced in him as compared to Mauclair or Michel. Clemenceau was entirely carried away and confessed inexhaustibly: "I cannot get rid of it. It obsesses me. I have to speak about it. And, for better or worse, I shall speak about it." Moreover, Clemenceau imagined the type of person who would enjoy the *Cathedral* series as much as he did to be a hedonist, and thus deserving of praise in Clemenceau's eyes: "One of these beings with two feet, whose principal merit is to wander around the earth with a pair of eyes ready to be carried away by all the feasts offered to us by the divine light."[7]

In other words, both Clemenceau and his adversaries saw in the spectator enjoying the Durand-Ruel show, somebody who lived for pleasure. While Mauclair and Michel sanctioned this moral extrapolation negatively, Clemenceau sanctioned it positively, placing himself at the opposite pole from Mauclair's puritanical, self-conscious reserve. It is interesting, however, that from both viewpoints, the *Cathedral* paintings seem to call for a redefinition of mankind: their impact on the viewer's senses shifts toward a compelling effort to analyze human nature.

It is also worth noting that both the Mauclair and Clemenceau interpretations of the *Cathedral* series are based on associating Monet's work with the connotations of paganism. Mauclair sees in it an "excessive" attempt, morally suspicious; Clemenceau sees there the opposite. Admiring Monet's Cathedrals becomes for Clemenceau the pretext to exalt Monet's "pagan", laical approach to life and to taunt the Church and its clerics: "While my feeble vicar tries to torture himself into becoming entranced with miracles that are not, I myself live within a perpetual wonder which frightens and inebriates me with miraculous realities. (...) Yes, humanity lives in a miracle, in a real miracle whence it can ceaselessly draw incredible joys: the only thing is that it does not notice it, or to be more precise, it only just starts to formulate the notion of it."[8]

Clearly, Mauclair installs his comment on the *Cathedrals* in the ideological context of the time; likewise, Clemenceau's anti-clericalism colours his own vision of Monet's paintings. Rouen Cathedral has lost all of its religious attributes and becomes the source of a sheer physical, visual enjoyment. From this, Clemenceau deduces that there is no need to search for miracles that do not exist. Instead, the miracles are to be found every day, every hour in the way Monet has recorded his shimmering, ecstatic sensations in front of the cathedral, although Clemenceau's interpretation takes little account of Monet's sufferings and his extended, painstaking efforts to produce the final result.

Clemenceau may have taken on the disguise of an art critic for a day, as he put it, but he did not part with the usual verbal rhetoric of a radical French parliamentarian at the end of last century. In his article, Clemenceau addressed the President of France, with an ill-concealed touch of arrogant cynicism: "And you, Félix Faure, my sovereign for a day, you who rule graciously in Mme. de Pompadour's [palace] with Roujon and Poincaré at your side to guide you in your art appreciation, I have read that you have made I-don't-know-what personal purchases at I-don't-know-what art market; that's your business. But you aren't just Félix Faure, you are the president of the Republic, and the French Republic at that. It's in this title, obviously, that you went the other day to visit Napoleon's night table, as if it were there that the great man had left his genius. How could you not have had, instead, the idea of going to look at the work of one of our contemporaries on whose account France will be celebrated throughout the world long after your name will have fallen into oblivion? What did Poincaré do, what did Roujon say? Could they have been invaded by the restoring sleep of Kaempfen? Don't awaken those good sleepers; and because there is in you a bit of fancy, go and look at this series of cathedrals, as the good bourgeois that you are, without asking anyone's opinion. Perhaps you might understand and, remembering that you represent France, perhaps you will consider endowing France with those twenty paintings that, together, represent a moment for art. . . ."[9]

Clemenceau's point, if overstated, was a valid one, and all the more so as it went almost totally unheard. Camondo was the only collector who gathered as many as five of Monet's *Cathedrals*, and subsequently gave them to the Louvre. Today, only one private collector owns more than one *Cathedral*. Only one museum owns more than two, the Musée d'Orsay which owns altogether six.

Some critics who viewed the 1895 show at Durand-Ruel felt compelled to recreate a certain order within the series – to align the paintings according to a certain *a posteriori* logic. To view the Cathedrals at random, to glance at one and then another arbitrarily, as one picks one poem and another out of a volume of poetry, seemed to be a possibility that must be excluded. There had to be a certain order to these twenty paintings, as Clemenceau clearly stated, and it was up to the viewer to reconstruct it: "Skilfully chosen, the twenty states of light, the twenty paintings are ordered, classified and completed in an achieved evolution."[10] Two systems of order retained attention; the first was a circular one (Clemenceau), the other was based on the model of a linear chain (Geffroy). The question of the order of the whole *Cathedral* series is intimately related to the question of the order of the twenty paintings in the 1895 exhibition, which should have reflected Monet's own notion of their possible sequence. The problem is made somewhat difficult by the fact that there are very few clues as to what the hanging of the 1895 exhibition looked like.

We can, however, proceed by elimination. We know to a certain extent what the exhibition did not look like; as Paul Tucker put it: "[Monet] certainly did not arrange the *Cathedrals* chronologically or according to weather conditions. Nor did he do it on the basis of when he may have begun or completed individual canvases." Tucker seems correct in suggesting that the order of the hanging was based "on visual relationships between pictures (...) and, most important, the colour schemes."[11] Indeed Tucker's suggestion is corroborated by Clemenceau's observations on the "achieved evolution" of the twenty *Cathedrals* exhibited in 1895.

This is what Clemenceau had to say about the order of the 1895 hanging: "Hung as they are, the twenty paintings are twenty marvellous revelations for us, but the narrow relation that ties them together escapes the fast observer, I'm afraid. Ordered according to their function, they could appear as the perfect equivalence of art and phenomena: the miracle."[12] Then Clemenceau, instead of giving a precise description of the exhibition sequence, proceeded to rehang the whole exhibition in his mind and prompted the reader who read his review to imagine the result: "Imagine them aligned on the four walls, as today, but serially, according to transitions of light: the great black mass in the beginning of the grey series constantly growing lighter, to the white series, going from the molten light to bursting precisions that continue and culminate in the fires of the rainbow series, which themselves subside in the calm of the blue series and fade away in the divine mist of azure.

"Then with one big, circular glance, you could have a stunning perception of the monster, a revelation of the marvel.

"And these grey cathedrals, which are purple or azure man-handled with gold; and these white cathedrals with porticos of fire, burning with green, red or blue flames; and these rainbow cathedrals that seem to be seen through a turning prism; and these blue cathedrals, which are pink, would give you all of a sudden the lasting vision, not of twenty, but of a hundred, of a thousand, of a million versions of the eternal cathedral in the immense cycle of the sun." Clemenceau's imaginative reconstruction simply concluded: "That's what I saw in Monet's Cathedrals, this is the way they should be arranged by Durand-Ruel in order to have them felt and understood in the harmony of their whole."[13]

A plausible suggestion of Clemenceau's imaginary rehanging of Monet's Cathedrals could be:

Grey series – four paintings: plates 2, 3, 13 and 30.
White series – six paintings: plates 5, 6, 7, 17, 23 and 29.
Rainbow series – four paintings: plates 15, 16, 18 and 28.
Blue series – six paintings: plates 1, 14, 19, 22 and 27.

This mental exercise conveys the effect of circularity described by Clemenceau with, for instance, plate 1 in the blue series hanging on the wall next to the grey series, where plate 2 would be hanging – the two paintings forming a pair. The overall division of twenty *Cathedrals* on four walls, into four groups of four, six, four and six paintings could only have enhanced the sense of harmony underscored in Clemenceau's description.

While Clemenceau's observations are interesting for the suggestion of an order of the *Cathedrals* based purely upon chromatic criteria, they do not contribute to a view of how the Durand-Ruel

exhibition truly appeared. An interesting review that has been given infrequent attention, by Henry Eon in *La Plume*, 1 June 1895[14] provides useful information on the actual arrangement of the Durand-Ruel show: "First there is the morning in the mist – the monument seems to be coming out of a cloud." (This can be read as a clear reference to plate 14.) "Then there is the grey pink morning: a light mist surrounds it." Eon then sharpens his description: "The façade remains in shadow; only the top of a tower emerges in the rising sun; as the bells of the angelus ring [at 7am], a flight of crows scatters through the sky." (Unmistakably, this passage records plates 27, 28 and 30.) "But then you see the portal seen frontally, very studied although without excessive detail. The same portal in grey weather has whitish and iridescent patina, and a velvet of rust has dressed the saints with capes, has put girdles around the trefoils of the spires and tatters of drapery on the small columns of the portico." (The "whitish" painting is probably plate 13, the iridescent effect, plate 3.) "Soon all these patinas vanish; the Cathedral stands out majestically under the big sun of noon – the sun that gilds, heats up and dresses the Cathedral with a very rich and very magnificent cape. It is no longer a church, it is a dazzling shrine." (This seems to refer to plates 5, 7, 22, 23 and 29.)

"The day goes on and the sun is setting. The blinding gold that the sun applied to the walls is now clinging to the corners of the cornices, protrusions, and gargoyles. The portal – this deserted, hermetically closed and mysterious portal, as silent as a grave forever sealed – goes back into the darkness." One can apparently read, in this highly lyrical and tendentiously symbolistic prose, a reference to the few paintings in which the portal seems to recede into the shade: plates 15 to 19. However, Eon here seems to misread the time of the day – the portal is in shadow not because of the sunset, which would fully illuminate the top of the west façade, but because these are mostly early morning paintings. The light falls on the cathedral from the east and leaves therefore the west façade largely unlit. As for plate 19, this is probably a painting executed around noon on a cloudy day. However, the pictorial interpretation in these works may have misled Eon in thinking that these were all sunset effects.

Eon then continued his review: "Let us follow the artist around the edifice. We arrive in the Cour de La Maitrise where the grey slate roofs are in harmony with the grey stones and rose-coloured lichens. Old houses, just like weary pilgrims, are leaning against the buttresses and seem to wait until they are asked to tell us the pious feelings of the past centuries." (Here he seems to refer to plates 1 and 2.) Finally, to close his tour around the show, Eon comes to the almost dematerialized view, plate 25: "Claude Monet owed it to his past fame to give us a foggy impression. He did not fail there, and he haunts us with a ghost-cathedral that seems to oscillate in a turbid atmosphere; the disappointed eye searches in vain to find a set point." This ends one of the most precise descriptions of the Durand-Ruel show, and yet one of the least examined contemporary accounts.

The selection of *Cathedrals* at Durand-Ruel is also revealing for the paintings it did not include; in particular, all of the sunset views of the Cathedral painted after 4pm from Louvet's (plates 8 to 12) were kept out of the exhibition. We can only speculate on why Monet excluded his evening paintings; those that he called his "gold and red motifs" in a letter to his wife in 1892. We can deduce from this that Monet was not primarily interested in recreating for the public the whole cycle of his day's work – the progression of the motifs at every moment of the day, from morning to twilight. He apparently favoured a chromatic arrangement, displaying works according to their prevailing colour.

It is noteworthy that in contrast to Clemenceau's classification, Geffroy gave priority to the succession of hours, although it is to be observed that Geffroy's text is much less rigorous and systematic than

Clemenceau's in its effort to categorize the *Cathedrals*[15]. "These works", commented Geffroy, "will give all the same sensation of the eternal beauty of life, present at every hour, at every moment. The reality is present and becomes transfigured. These pinnacles, these portals, these buttresses, these Rouen sculptures, all that stone seen at every hour of the day, in the softness of the morning, in the illumination of noon, seen under all the aspects of the atmosphere, under the caress of the sun, through the opacity of the fog or the air loaded with rain." "What Monet paints is the space that exists between him and things", states Geffroy, echoing Monet's own description. "He sets up his bright dream of clarity in front of himself through these Rouen stones, whereupon he fixes all the wandering poetry summarized in these greenish shadows, in these luminous glitters, in these pink embers and these pure flames of gold."

Geffroy then proceeded to give his more detailed perception of the progression of each group of paintings: "The Rouen Cathedral, its tall shape erect on the ground, losing itself, vanishing into the bluish morning mist" describes the first group that Geffroy distinguishes among the series. We can certainly recognize here plates 14 and 25, and probably 26 to 28 as well.

"The portal dug like a marine grotto, the stone eroded by time turned gold and green by sun, moss and lichens." One can recognize a number of paintings in these lines, but in particular plates 7 and 23, and also 8 and 22. In the first two, the green highlights underscoring the edge and offsetting the sun-scorched façade make Geffroy's allusion unmistakable. All these works depict noon or early afternoon effects.

"The high façade taken over by the shade at its base, its peak lit up by sunlight, illuminated by that dying pink glitter." This is clearly a reference to the obvious sunset effects in plates 8 to 12. Reference to paintings that were not included in the Durand-Ruel show indicates that Geffroy must have written his text before the selection of works was made. Geffroy must therefore have reviewed the whole series of thirty paintings prior to the show, most certainly in Monet's studio in Giverny, and most likely wrote his text from his personal notes.

The texts on the *Cathedrals* by Clemenceau and Geffroy have become almost as famous as their subject. It is however, equally gratifying to look at the journalistic response to the *Cathedral* series, in particular as it reveals the range of contemporary perceptions of the Durand-Ruel retrospective. A vast array of newspapers carried reviews of the show. *Le Matin* of 10 May 1895 ran an unsigned article: "*Claude Monet chez Durand-Ruel – Le maitre impressionniste – Un doué.* The first mention of Monet refers to his "systematic abstention from the salons and the kind of indifference that he professes for the judgement of the hoi polloi." It is terribly important to remember that Monet, even though his success was firmly established, was still considered a rebel against the official artistic establishment, and that his vision and conception of reality was clearly not shared by everyone. The *Cathedrals* were, in that sense, described by the reviewer of *Le Matin* as an "answer to the bitter criticisms against the impressionists" that were still heard loud and clear. The article concluded: "the answer is extraordinary" and added this final laudatory note: "One should envy a man so perfectly gifted, and one should in particular feel sorry for those who do not understand his superiority."

Monet did not only encounter criticism from the ranks of official artists. George Moore, himself a defender of Impressionism, objected to the "feat" of painting "views of the Cathedral without once having recourse to the illusion of distance", and to the textured appearance of the coloured surface, which was "that of stone and mortar."[16]

Despite vast public acclaim for the *Cathedrals*, one of the most commonly heard criticisms was, essentially, that Monet had gone too far. Thadée Natanson interestingly expressed this opinion, describing

the *Cathedrals* as "an experimental and theoretical research through which the painter came up with too extreme a systematization of the process of series."[17] The same echo can be found in the lyrical, symbolistic approach of Ary Renan[18]: "The whims and the discipline of the brush have never been more strangely disturbing in Claude Monet's *oeuvre*." Renan explained his disturbance with an "impasto that was synthetic to the extreme, brutal and yet gentle", while sustaining "these ambiguous visions."

Another noticeable aspect of the abundant journalistic literature reviewing the Durand-Ruel show is a clear tendency to articulate Monet's *Cathedrals* through the symbolistic fashion in literary circles of the time; which often resulted in an effort from the reviewer to create a "literary" equivalent (infrequently successful) of the *Cathedrals* in his own text – thus one may be perplexed at some of the "metaphors" resorted to. According to Louis Lumet, the *Cathedrals* "exalt or darken the magical flight of the hours." Further on, Lumet elaborates: "Under the cool caress of the morning light, there is the portal in the subtle air, the stone turned pink, moved by the awakening of life; then the sun arises, the coloured tones swell in a crescendo scale until they reach the radiant and noisy shining of noon."[19]

Lumet, however, ends his article with a reference to the criticisms and sneers of the academic painters, as though over-the-top lyricism seemed the only alternative to downright slander: "Without giving in, without fooling himself, despite the sneers of the fools, and the anger of the painters who have invested interests and hold shops under the porch of the academies, [Claude Monet] is a proud and strong artist."[20]

Thadée Natanson also succumbs to the highly lyrical tone in favour at the time. He, however, raises questions about the *Cathedrals* that were not asked by his contemporaries, most importantly, the question of the subject matter in relation to the rest of Monet's work: "It seems that there is a certain bias, almost jealousy, in choosing a new site where nothing distracts from the worship of light."[21] Natanson was also the only critic at the time, to point out that Monet had decided to paint a subject that was itself a work of art, so that he could "dedicate himself more readily to that light – a subject which is preponderant in all his works so far, and which is unique" with the *Cathedrals*. In addition, Natanson sees in the *Cathedrals* the ultimate degree in the "pursuit of formulae to render the impression of light",[22] except that he imagines the next logical step might only be for Monet to paint a "cube of stone".

The climax of all lyricism found in the reviews of the 1895 show took the shape of an extraordinary, and almost embarrassing, poem written by Georges Demoinville, to celebrate the "mystical charm" of the Cathedrals.[23] Even though anecdotal, this is worth quoting as a measure of the prodigious variety of cultural responses generated by the *Cathedrals* in the press at the time:

"– Beautiful with a mystic beauty suggesting the hours of forgiveness and of foregone memory at the threshold of impregnable church squares.

– Magnificent in their dazzling splendour and their dazzling metamorphoses

– Triumphant, untameable in the august dignity of their sacred pillars,

– Temples of faith! Basilicas of Love!

– Disturbing apparitions, in the heavenly clouds,

– Only true shelters of our ancient sorrows and of our joys to come.

– Glowing symbols of our destinies.

– Radiant poem! Mysterious teaching from eternal sorrows and from promised redemptions

– Magical apotheosis of religion and dream."

In the *Indépendance belge*, Hippolyte Fierens-Gevaert in more sober style, also found an equivalence between the *Cathedrals* and poetry: "The magnificent poem", he wrote, "that Claude Monet devotes to the Cathedral of Rouen, sheds light on our mysterious relationships with the 'infinite detail of things';" Fierens-Gevaert explained: "the large sculpted portals of the church probably open on the Unknown. Nobody enters there."[24] And again, Frantz Jourdain also could not resist drawing a parallel between the *Cathedral* series and a poem: "These twenty canvases are held together, and coordinated. They form a formidable epic poem in which the old basilica becomes animated and receives a soul."[25]

Debate for and against the *Cathedrals* remained quite strong for several decades. Louis Vauxcelles, the art critic who was chiefly responsible for coining the labels of both Fauvism and Cubism, asked the following question: "At the bottom, is that method of the series anything else than an uninterrupted suite of recordings? Do these trials reach any final result? The order, the rhythm necessarily are missing; the composition is deliberately eliminated; has not any depth therefore gone? Where is here [in the series] the element of the meditation always present in Giotto, in Durer, in Tintoretto, in Nicolas Poussin, in Eugene Delacroix? To feel the world is not enough to be a great artist, one must also think it." Vauxcelles, in the same article, claims to want something else out of a painting than "sheer material reflections on a retina." "We want to know," he explained, "what the painter, and through him the man of this time, thinks of the world into which we have been thrown." Vauxcelles voiced here the first openly critical statement against Monet's series for being devoid of any human presence, and for being too concerned with rendering "the coloured texture of phenomena."[26]

The argument that Monet's technique in front of the cathedral was somewhat contrived and artificial did not die out easily. In 1927, with Monet recently dead, the debate continued: "Something systematic can be felt in these series sometimes which spoils them; and in particular, it seems that Monet despite all his genius, attempted there an unfeasible work. Was it possible, in front of the magnificent portal of one of our great cathedrals, to indulge oneself only in the gamut of light effects on the thousands of decorative reliefs?"[27] We witness here another example of a surreptitious shift of emphasis from an aesthetic criticism (the near impossibility of completing such a vast task) to an ethical judgement (this is betraying the glory of our Cathedral). Not only is the Cathedral series impossible but furthermore it is condemnable. The penchant toward seeing excesses of all kinds in Monet's *Cathedrals* was not infrequent in the mainstream of art criticism in the 1930s.

Roger Fry saw Monet's achievement as too rigorous and "scientific", to the point of ruining his artistic achievement: Monet's sole concern was, according to Fry, the atmospheric effects, and through this he had "lost all possibility of any definite formal design. (...) Monet cared only to reproduce on his canvas the actual visual sensation as far as that was possible. Perhaps if one had objected to him that this was equivalent to abandoning art, (...) he would have been unmoved because he aimed almost exclusively at a scientific documentation of appearances."[28]

This is an extraordinary judgement on the part of Fry, outcasting the *Cathedrals* and all of Monet's series as being on the fringe of "non-art". This merciless severity recalls the earlier condemnation of a German historian "that the painter's efforts to test the fertility of his method on a large scale and in different directions had resulted only in trivialities."[29] This writer accused Monet of having reduced the impressionist principle to absurdity. J.J. Sweeney associated Monet's plastic initiative with journalism, according to him "the equivalent of Zola's scrupulousness of *reportage* in literature." Sweeney explained his opinion: "This shift of interest from structural integrity, like the decay of faith in other walks of life, had left the artist without any sound basis. The encouragement of a scientific, detached impassivity struck directly at any link with emotions. And

in a conscientiously *reportorial* notation of natural phenomena there was no place for imagination or fantasy."[30]

Even Lionello Venturi was less than laudatory about Monet's *Cathedrals*: "The cathedrals are the most evident indication of Monet's creative decadence; in the *Haystacks* there was no question of form, but Rouen Cathedral possesses a very definite form and Monet's painting tries to preserve it and fails."[31]

Among contemporary reviews of the *Cathedrals* exhibition at Durand-Ruel, some of the most determining observations came from Monet's close colleagues. What they had to say was distinctly different from what the professional reviewers saw in the show. The observations of these artists, in the end, also had far more important repercussions than the occasionally somewhat hackneyed remarks of some critics.

The first mention was by Boudin, who had initiated Monet in *plein air* painting thirty years previously. Boudin, in a letter to his pupil Braquaval, commented thus on the event at Durand-Ruel: "Something interesting to see: the exhibition of the Monets at Durand-Ruel. You will see there paintings of quite strange character; it is a suite of views of Rouen Cathedral under different aspects, very rich in colours and with wonderful *empasto*. Although everyone does not approve of either the procedure or the way of looking, there is here quite a strange interpretation, and something finely detailed and pushed to the limits of technique."[32]

Pissarro could not hide his unreserved enthusiasm. On 11 May 1895 he announced the event to his son Lucien: "Monet has just opened his exhibition yesterday: there will be twenty *Cathedrals of Rouen*!!!! forty canvases altogether. This is going to be 'the great attraction'. It will last until the end of the month."[33] A week later Pissarro reminds Lucien that he should try to come back from England to France in time to see the *Cathedrals*, and in the letter refers to the controversial reviews: "Monet exhibits his *Cathedrals* until May 31. Try to be back in time to see them; there is much noise about them. It is the subject of much controversy among some and greatly admired by others."[34]

Pissarro's testimony is interesting in three ways: it echoes the importance of the event within the media and for the artists themselves; it gives us some idea of the polarization of the debate and of the controversy that ensued from the exhibition; and it provides some account of how fellow artists responded. There is further enthusiasm in a letter Pissarro wrote to his second son Georges: "The Monet exhibition makes big noise in Paris. The young painter Anquetin and company allege that this is not painting, that anybody can do it. In fact, he [Monet] is simply an admirable artist – it will be seen this way later on! More than ever the impressionists are controversial."[35]

On 26 May, Camille Pissarro wrote again to Lucien: "I regret that you cannot be here before the closing of the Monet exhibition; his *Cathedrals* are going to be scattered to one side and another, and it is particularly as a whole that they must be seen. (...) It is very much fought against by the younger ones and even by some admirers of Monet. I am very much taken by this extraordinary mastery. Cézanne, whom I met yesterday at Durand-Ruel's, quite agrees with me in that this is the work of a headstrong individual, it is well balanced, and pursues the imperceptible nuance of effects that I have seen executed by no other artist. A few artists refute the necessity of this investigation; personally, I find all investigation justifiable when it is felt to this extent."[36]

In yet another letter, (1 June) Pissarro puts astonishing emphasis on the exhibition, its impact both for himself and for others: "It closes on June 4, and the twenty *Cathedrals* will be dispersed. Yet with a small effort, you could have been here in time. It is a great pity, for the *Cathedrals* are fiercely debated, and also much praised by Degas, myself, Renoir and others. I so much wish that you had seen these as a whole, for I find in them a superb unity which I have long sought."[37] Pissarro had made one more trip to Paris just to see the *Cathedrals* again. Eventually the exhibition, having received so much attention, was extended until June 8, and Lucien was back from London in time to view the paintings.

A very useful account of the reactions of the painters of the generation succeeding the Impressionists can be found in John Rewald's presentation of Paul Signac's *Journal*.[38] Theo van Rysselberghe was quite "taken by the execution" of the *Cathedrals*. According to him, "Monet is there altogether, with his qualities and his flaws, each of these stronger than ever – one has to take him or leave him."[39] Henry Edmond Cross, Maximilien Luce and Paul Signac found on the whole that the *Cathedrals* left the viewer unsatisfied. Cross remarked that the whole thing looked like a "tiered cake".[40] Luce, who had already expressed his disenchantment with the *Cathedrals* to Pissarro,[41] is reported by Signac as having passed the following verdict: "[Monet's] qualities as a painter do not seem strong enough to justify the lack of composition."[42]

Surprisingly it was with subsequent generations of painters outside of France that the *Cathedrals* found their most unequivocal admirers. This was certainly true of the German impressionists Slevogt, Corinth, Liebermann, and Zorn.[43] But perhaps the most significant and the most emblematic response was that of Kasimir Malevich: "The *Cathedral of Rouen* is of capital importance for the history of art and, by the strength of its action, forces whole generations to change their conceptions."[44] What appeared to be of primary concern to Malevich was, predictably, Monet's relative indifference to his subject matter. "In the *Cathedral of Rouen*," wrote Malevich, "we do not see that the painter took care to render the images [of the painted object]." The theme of the cathedral itself "is not so important, with regard to the pictorial relationships, and to the changes of coloured elements. For most people, such paintings, with all their changes, are not worth anything because they do not depict the world in a concrete manner."[45]

If it is common knowledge that Monet's *Haystacks* were the precursors of Wassily Kandinsky's first abstract paintings, the direct relationship between Monet's *Cathedrals* and Malevich's suprematist images seems to have been somewhat overlooked. Malevich was also keen to perceive the *Cathedrals* outside the traditional framework of "bourgeois religious ideology." "It is not possible to say that Claude Monet has reflected bourgeois religious ideology in the *Cathedral of Rouen*, and this is because Monet worked first and foremost on the predominantly physical change of light."[46] Lastly, referring to the famous "lichens" on which some critics of the 1890s dwelt somewhat heavily, Malevich found a metaphor for the *Cathedrals* worth quoting: "If pictorial plants on the walls of a cathedral were indispensable for Monet, the body of the Cathedral was considered by him as flower

beds on whose surface the paint that it needed would grow."[47]

Monet's *Cathedrals* having had such a determining impact on one of the chief founders of non-figurative painting before World War I, it is no great surprise that Jackson Pollock, in the forefront of non-figurative painting during and after World War II, also looked at Monet's *Cathedrals*. The witness of Pollock's interest here is not a text, but a painting entitled Cathedral, described as "one of his most gestural canvases."[48] Roy Lichtenstein found in Monet's *Cathedrals* a source of pictorial reflection for Pop Art. What interested him chiefly, it seems, was the repetitive aspect of the technique, and the reproductive mechanism of one image after another: "The *Cathedrals*," Lichtenstein explained, "are meant to be manufactured Monets – it's an industrial way of making impressionism, or something like it, by a machine-like technique. But it probably takes me ten times as long to do one of the Cathedrals as it took Monet to do his, (...) although Monet painted his *Cathedrals* as a series, which is a very modern idea, the image was painted slightly differently in each painting. So I thought using three slightly different images in three different colours as a play on different times of the day would be more interesting (...) They deal with the impressionist cliché of not being able to read the image close up; it becomes clearer as you move away from it."[49]

It seems that until the *Cathedrals*, and the later Monets, underwent a more or less complete "rehabilitation", to use Clement Greenberg's expression[50] in the late 1950s, critics' views of the *Cathedral* series relied on a curious double paradox. There seemed to be little room for any other approach than either deprecating Monet's *Cathedrals* as extreme or excessive, hence abusive or even blasphemous, or exalting "mystical beauty", and thus being totally carried away by its grandiose mystery. These alternatives left little scope for any attempt to analyse what the Cathedrals were about. Their narrow and constricting opposition lasted far longer than one might imagine, and probably explained why it was not until the late 1950s and early 60s that the first serious efforts to understand the *Cathedrals* were achieved, notably by George Heard Hamilton and subsequently by Daniel Wildenstein who for the first time with the publication of his *Catalogue Raisonné* made us understand how many *Cathedrals* are in existence today.

This late departure to a proper effort towards critical analysis of the *Cathedrals* is all the more surprising in view of the impact of the *Cathedrals* on successive generations of painters, and among them representatives of the most important movements of twentieth-century art. But it was from an artist, not a critic, that Monet received the most immediate and perceptive contemporary response to his achievement in the *Cathedral* series; from his colleague Camille Pissarro, whose letters celebrate unequivocally the astonishing range and impact of the *Cathedral* paintings, of "effects that I have seen executed by no other artist."

EPILOGUE

There is an interesting relation between the response to the *Cathedrals* and the way the late works of Cézanne were perceived. The same Mauclair who detected "blasphemy" in Monet's *Cathedrals* found Cézanne's colours "brutal and discordant".[1] The rearguard of critics of both Monet and Cézanne saw excess and abuse in the former's works, coarseness and madness in the latter's. The judgement was, however, completely reversed in the case of Cézanne, essentially due to the emergence of Cubism, which prompted critics to reassess Cézanne's works and evolve new idioms with which to discuss his achievements.

No such thing happened as far as the *Cathedrals* were concerned. While the 1895 show at Durand-Ruel enjoyed a wide *succès d'estime*, the *Cathedrals* were seen by subsequent generations of critics as the last thing that nineteenth-century French painting had to say. By contrast, the late work of Cézanne came to be viewed as the first major 'statement' of twentieth-century painting. It is a tantalizing thought that in 1895 when the *Cathedrals* were first exhibited, any spectator could also have seen, in that same year, the centenary exhibition honouring Corot and the first Vollard exhibition of Cézanne's work. Retrospectively, Corot's works could be regarded as intrinsically revealing the virtues of nineteenth-century French landscape painting, Monet's as the definitive and final contribution to what Corot had established, and Cézanne's as preparing for what painting was to become in the forthcoming century.

Yet, if we accept this uncompromising distinction between the significant historical functions of Monet's *Cathedrals* and Cézanne's late works, we can still identify a shared goal conceived independently by the two artists. This has to do both with the pictorial concerns that they addressed and their solutions to them, and the challenges that they posed to the artistic conventions of their time.

Liliane Brion-Guerry, in a beautiful article explained that: "If in the history of spatial composition, in the continuity of its expression, Cézanne constitutes "the great divide", if he can be said to stand at the beginning of all modern painting, Cubism, Expressionism, abstraction – it is because he 'dismantled space', overturning an order that had lasted for four centuries of Western painting. Cézannian space is no longer a cube of air inside which volumes are laid out in accordance with a pre-established arrangement, where it is possible within a given structure to alter the position and form of a figurative object, so long as it is rationally integrated with a traditional system of representation. In Cézanne's composition, unlike that which obeys the laws and methods of Alberti's perspective (classical perspective, which despite all the transfigurations of the Baroque, prevailed in Western painting until Impressionism), the spatial container (. . .) does not exist prior to its contents and is not distinct from them; it is on the very existence of the latter that the whole figurative construction depends. It is the object (. . .) that by expanding in the third dimension gives rise by itself to the proper structure that will bestow its identity. This object thus finds itself, by its very nature, indissolubly bound to the "space it engenders and from which it will never be able to dissociate itself." Brion-Guerry rightly argued that Cézannian space is no longer space indifferent to its contents (. . .) it is a world in itself where objects and their interstices are immediate data."[2]

One can make the contention here that Monetian space, as perceived in the *Cathedrals*, and Cézannian space, as described above, offer definite analogies. Despite the different methods and pictorial interpretations of the two artists, they worked along parallel lines in some respects. Monet's *Cathedrals* certainly did their share in "overturning (. . .) a traditional system of representation". What is described in relation to Cézanne as "the spatial container" corresponds to what Monet called the *enveloppe*. This, too, does not "exist prior to its contents" – the *enveloppe* is indissolubly bound to the cathedral. Mirbeau expressed this in clear terms: "between our eyes and the appearance of figures (. . .) the air intervenes in a real sense."[3] Monet explained in relation to the *Haystacks* the perception that culminated in the *Cathedrals*: "For me, a landscape does not exist in its own right, since its appearance changes at every moment; but its surroundings bring it to life – the air and the light, which vary continually (. . .) for me it is only the surrounding atmosphere which gives objects their real value."[4]

The last recorded meeting between Cézanne and Monet took place in Giverny, on Monet's invitation, when Cézanne came for lunch in company with Clemenceau, Rodin, Geffroy and Mirbeau on 28 November 1894.[5] It is difficult to imagine that the *Cathedrals*, which Monet was just finishing, would not have been one of the subjects of discussion at that meeting. At this point, Monet and Cézanne were each involved in forging an extremely individual pictorial idiom that would convey a radical approach to the concept of 'reality'.

Much of the problem that perhaps has somehow concealed the factor of profound innovation in the *Cathedrals* is their portrayal as the last remnant of an essentially positivistic perception about space and time: that is, that the *Cathedrals* reflect "a presentation of visual phenomena seen from a given position in space at a given moment in time."[6] In the context of this interpretation, Impressionism appears as the ultimate refinement of the perception and depiction of space as restricted to the place here, and of time as restricted to the moment now. In that sense, Impressionism seems rooted in Comte's assertion that "there is an immutable necessity in the external world (. . .) an invariable order actually existing without us (. . .) All events, whatever the events of our personal and social life included, are always subject to natural relations of sequence and similitude, which in all essential respects lie beyond the reach of our interference."[7]

According to George Heard Hamilton, "despite their technical subtlety, the *Cathedrals*, for this spectator at least, are the last even though they may be the finest demonstrations of a point of view toward the representation of space and time which assumes as a fundamental principle that physical nature is all that exists, that it is the limit of experience and knowledge, that nature is of universal extension, self-contained and determined through and through by the laws of causal necessity."[8] Hamilton's analysis of the fairly uniform and altogether simple conceptual complexion of the *Cathedrals* is based on the premise that "the observer [Monet] is outside time and space (. . .) within the painting all positions are established as a series of intricate but fixed relations to the observer and to each other. Similarly, all these positions exist simultaneously in relation to each other, and with or without the observer. Despite such superficial sensational evidence of time as the description of climate, weather, season of the year and hour of the day, Impressionist space is essentially timeless since it exists only in terms of the instant at which it is observed." Thus, the *Cathedrals* would finally seem "to indicate that the immediate data of perception have been recorded within a conventional, pre-determined pictorial order."[9]

Hamilton's profound understanding of the *Cathedrals* can be heeded as a cornerstone of the comprehension of Monet's edifice. The conclusion to be drawn in this book, however, is precisely the reverse of Hamilton's analysis. As has been emphasized in an earlier chapter, the problem of time is absolutely central to the making of the *Cathedrals*. Monet, while struggling with the ceaselessly changing time and weather, working on as many as twelve canvases in one day to keep up with the range of visual sensations, cannot be seen as an observer who stood "outside time and space".

Further, the *Cathedral* series is founded on a dual unresolvable notion of time: the time of the observer (what Hamilton called "momentaneous time") watching the cathedral under the effect of an instant; and the time of the painter (what Hamilton called "extended time" and omitted to see in the *Cathedrals*) during which the painter applies the paint to his canvas, endeavouring to catch the effect of his observation. These two times are not identical to each other, nor are they the reflection of each other. Yet Monet's task was to superimpose them. The time through which Monet passed in painting his *Cathedrals* was not a smooth, homogeneous and continuous time, it was broken time incorporating intensity, waste, interruption; full of uncertainties, constructions, reconstructions and failures. Monet's single recurring obsession in front of his cathedral was not to waste time in his race with the weather, and yet, he could not but waste time. The time of the Cathedrals was reconstructed, through time, around a single event: the observation of an effect, followed by the pictorial, durational effect of an observation.

The most radical discovery that Monet perhaps ended in making was to observe, intentionally or not, that the apparent continuum of time is in effect made up of different types of time. The time of the *Cathedrals*, as one reads Monet's letters, as one passes from one image to another, seems plural and irregular, manifold and variable. Thinking about time was, therefore, essentially constitutive of the *Cathedrals*. It was not however, a monolithic conception of time, but one filled with knots and complexities; one more appropriate to a pictorial account of an artistic struggle.

FOOTNOTES

INTRODUCTION

1. George Moore, *Modern Painting*, London, 1893, p. 84. Moore further insisted that "Monet is the only painter to whom [this definition] can be reasonably applied."
2. R.R. Bernier, "The subject and painting: Monet's ‹‹ language of the sketch››", *Art History*, Vol. 12, no. 3, Sept. 1989, p. 298–321. Routledge & Kegan Paul.
3. Emile Cardon, "La Presse des revoltes", in *La Presse*, 29 April, 1874, p. 263. Quoted by R.R. Bernier, *loc. cit.* p. 301. Routledge & Kegan Paul.
4. R.R. Bernier, *loc. cit.* p. 303.
5. R.R. Bernier, *loc. cit.* p. 318.

ORIGINS OF THE CATHEDRAL SERIES

1. Christopher Lloyd, "Camille Pissarro and Rouen" in *Studies on Camille Pissarro*, London, New York, 1986, p. 75. Routledge & Kegan Paul.
2. Gustave Geffroy, *Monet, Sa Vie et Son Oeuvre*, Paris, 1980, p. 188 (first published in 1924). (Translation by the author). Macula.
3. *cf.* Christopher Lloyd, "Camille Pissarro and Rouen" in *Studies on Camille Pissarro*, London, New York, 1986, p. 91, note 17, with acknowledgement to Richard Brettell.
4. A. de Lostalot, "Exposition des Oeuvres de M. Claude Monet", in *Gazette des Beaux-Arts*, 1883, Vol. I, p. 342–348.
5. *cf.* D. Wildenstein, *Claude Monet: Biographie et Catalogue Raisonné*, Vol. II, p. Bibliotheque des Arts, Lausanne.
6. Janine Bailly-Herzberg, *Correspondance de Camille Pissarro*, Paris, 1980, Vol. I, p. 184. Presses Universitaires de France.
7. *cf.* Camille Pissarro's letter written to Lucien from Rouen, 20 November 1883 (J.B.H. Vol. I, p.253): "Je viens de terminer ma serie de peintures, je les regarde beaucoup."
8. *cf.* M. Melot, "A Rebel's Role", in *Studies on Camille Pissarro* p. 120. Routledge & Kegan Paul.
9. John House, *Monet – Nature into Art*, New Haven and London, 1986, p. 226–227. Yale University Press.
10. Michel Melot, "La pratique de l'artiste: Pissarro graveur en 1880", *Histoire et Critique des Arts*, June 1977, p. 14–31.
11. *Ibid.*, p. 15.
12. Theodore Robinson, Diary, 1892–1896, Frick Art Reference Library, for 23 May 1892; quoted by Grace Seiberling, *Monet's Series*, Garland Press, New York, 1981, p. 137.
13. Michel Melot, *op. cit.* p. 17. *Histoire et Critique des Arts*.
14. *cf.* Grace Seiberling, *op. cit.* p. 134: "Monet already had the idea of painting the Cathedral when he set out for Rouen and apparently planned to stay there for some time, although he could not have anticipated how long it would take him to complete the paintings, nor how much anguish they would cause him. Previously, sequences had resulted from his travels or his experiences; now the decision to paint a series preceded his departure for the motif."
15. Janine Bailly-Herzberg, *op. cit.* Vol. I, p. 243

16. G.H. Hamilton, *Claude Monet's Paintings of Rouen Cathedral*, London, 1960, p. 13. Oxford University Press.
17. *Ibid.*, p. 26, with a quotation of Pierre Francastel, *L'Impressionnisme*, 1937, p. 93.
18. Victor Merlhes, *Correspondance de Paul Gauguin, documents temoignages*, Paris, 1984, p. 106.
19. *Ibid*, p. 107.
20. Janine Bailly-Herzberg, *Correspondance de Camille Pissarro*, Vol. I, p. 252. Pissarro is referring to a drawing by Turner and to a lithograph by Bonington (Curtis 16) *Voyages Pittoresques et romantiques dans l'ancienne France*, Paris, Vol. II, 1824.

MONET IN FRONT OF THE CATHEDRAL

1. *cf.* Wildenstein, Vol. III, p. 50.
2. *cf.* Wildenstein, Vol. III, p. 46.
3. Monet is hinting at the fact that when he was painting his poplars, he had to buy the whole field where the poplars stood, in order to save the trees from being sold to a wood dealer.
4. Presumably one in each venue, now Mauquit's and Louvet's.
5. As he wrote these lines, Monet most probably could remember having seen the works by his disciple, friend and recent witness at his wedding, Paul Helleu. Helleu had done a group of works evocative of the iridescent and trembling light of the stained glass windows studied from inside the Cathedral.
6. G.H. Hamilton, op. cit. p. 16.
7. Ibid. p. 15–16.
All citations of letters refer to Daniel Wildenstein's *Claude Monet: Biographie et Catalogue Raisonné*, Vol. III,

MOTIF AND SERIES

1. Quoted by Felibien, *Entretiens sur les vies et les ouvrages des plus excellent Peintures anciens et modernes*, London, 1705, Vol IV, p.iii, quoted by Louis Marin, "Towards a theory of reading", Calligram, Cambridge 1988, p.67. Charles Le Brun, who himself painted a series of paintings depicting the life of Alexander the Great, ruled the Académie Royale de Peinture et de Sculpture, founded in 1648 by Louis XIV.
2. Louis Marin, *ibid.*

THE SIGNIFICANCE OF THE GOTHIC

1. Gregory of Tours, *Liber de Cursa Stellarum, Monumenta Germaniae Historica, Scriptorum rerum Merovingicarum*, I, 875 ff; quoted by Walter Cahn, *Masterpieces*, Princeton, 1979, p. 29. Princeton University Press, Princeton N.J.
2. Henri Omont, "Les sept merveille du monde du Moyen Age", quoted by Walter Cahn, *op. cit.* p. 30. Princeton University Press.
3. Eugene Boudin, excerpt from his notebooks, *c.* 1854–59 in G. Jean-Aubry, *Eugene Boudin*, Paris, 1922, p. 29.
4. Although this aspect of Renoir as a theoretician of architecture is seldom mentioned in the literature available on Renoir, mention can be found of it in Jean Renoir's; *Memoirs: Auguste*

Renoir, Folio Gallimard, p. 258.
5. *Ibid.*, p. 261
6. *Ibid.*, p. 262
7. Wildenstein, *op. cit.* Vol. III, letters no. 1208.
8. Janine Bailly-Herzberg, *op. cit.* Vol I, p. 252. Presses Universitaires de France.
9. Janine Bailly-Herzberg, "Camille Pissarro and Rouen", *L'oeil*, July-August 1981, nos. 312–313.
10. J.B.H. Vol. IV, p. 266. Editions du Valhermeil.
11. Quoted by Janine Bailly-Herzberg, "Camille Pissarro et Rouen", *L'oeil*, July-August, 1981, nos. 312–313, p. 58.
12. cf. Richard Brettell, Christopher Lloyd, *A Catalogue of the Drawings by Camille Pissarro in the Ashmolean Museum*, Oxford, 1980, p. 149, no. 158c (illustrated). Oxford University Press.
13. Emile Mâle, *L'Art religieux du XIII siecle en France Etude sur l'iconographie du Moyen Age et sur ses sources d'inspiration*, Paris, 1898, trans. Princeton, 1984. *Religious Art in France*, p. 3. Princeton University Press, Princeton, J.H. (U.S.) – Guildford, Surrey (U.K.) (Bollingen Series)
14. Otto von Simson, *op cit.*, p. 3.
14a. Monet to Clemenceau quoted by D. Cooper in *Claude Monet*, Catalogue p. 16, 1957, Tate Gallery.
15. Emile Mâle, *op. cit.*, p. 32.
16. *Ibid.*
17. Emile Mâle, *loc. cit.*, p. 32.
18. J.B. Deperthes, *Histoire de l'art du paysage*, Paris, 1822, p. 312; quoted by Albert Boime, *The Academy and French Painting in the XIXth Century*, N.H., London, 1986, p. 141. Yale University Press.
19. Otto von Simson, *op cit.*, p. 3.
20. *Ibid.*
21. *Ibid.*
22. *Ibid.*
23. For this analysis on the signification of light in Medieval Gothic architecture, see, in particular, Georges Duby, *Le temps des Cathedrales, l'art et la societe, 980–1420*, Paris, 1976, p. 121–162.
24. *Ibid.*
25. Quoted by Georges Duby, *op. cit.*, p. 127.
26. Wildenstein, *op. cit.*, vol. III, p. 227, letter no. 825.
27. *Ibid.*, p. 247, letter no. 971.
28. Otto von Simson, *op. cit.*, p. 50.
29. *cf.* Emile Mâle, *op. cit.*, p.7.
30. *Ibid.*
31. *Ibid.*
32. *Ibid.*
33. Quoted by Emile Mâle, *op. cit.*, p. 352.
34. Emile Mâle, *op. cit.*, p. 353.

CATHEDRALS AND CRITICS

1. G.H. Hamilton, *Claude Monet's Paintings of Rouen Cathedral*, London, 1960, Oxford University Press p. 26.

2. Oscar Reutersward, *Monet*, Stockholm, 1948, quoted in *Monet: a retrospective*, ed. by C. Stuckey, Galley Press p. 171–172.

3. C.Mauclair, "Choses d'Art", in *Mercure de France*, June 1895, p. 357.

4. Andre Michel, *Notes sur l'Art Moderne*, (*Peinture*), Paris, Armand Colin, 1896

5. *Ibid.*

6. C. Mauclair, *op. cit.*

7. Georges Clemenceau, "Revolution des Cathédrales", in *Grand Pan*, 1896, Fasquelle, Paris, p. 428.

8. Georges Clemenceau, *Ibid.*, p. 429.

9. Translation by Charles Stuckey in *Monet: a retrospective*, ed. by C. Stuckey, Galley Press, p. 180.

10. G. Clemenceau in Stuckey, *op. cit.* p. 179..

11. *cf.* Paul Tucker, *op. cit.*, p. 279, note 39. Tucker ends this surmise on the order of the 1895 hanging with the following cautionary note: "Any theories about the installation, however, must remain tentative, given the lack of secure documentation." Yale University Press.

12. Clemenceau, *op. cit.*, cf. Stuckey, *op. cit.* p. 179.

13. *Ibid.*

14. Henry Eon, "Les Cathédrales de Claude Monet", in *La Plume*, 1 June 1895, p. 259.

15. Gustave Geffroy, *Monet: Sa vie, Son Oeuvre*, Editions Macula, Paris, 1980, p. 336–7.

16. George Moore, *Modern Painting*, 1898, p. 248.

17. Thadée Natanson, in *La Revue Blanche*, 1, June 1895, p. 521–523; quoted by H. Adhémar in *Hommage à Claude Monet*, p. 294.

18. Ary Renan, "Petites exposition: 50 tableaux de M. Claude Monet" in *Chronique des arts et de la curiosite*, 18 May 1895, p. 184.

19. Louis Lumet, "Sensations d'art (C.M.), la cathedrale de Rouen" *L'Enclos*, June 1895.

20. *Ibid.*

21. Thadée Natanson, *La Revue Blanche*, 1 June 1895, p. 521.

22. *Ibid.*

23. Georges Demoinville, "Les Salons, les cathédrales (de Claude Monet)", in *Journal des Artistes*, 19 May 1895.

24. Hippolyte Fierens-Gevaert, "Chronique artistique de Paris. Exposition des oeuvres de Corot et de Claude Monet" in *Indépendance Belge*, 20 June 1895.

25. Frantz Jourdain, "Les Salons; Exposition de Claude Monet chez Durand-Ruel" in *La Patrie*, 20 May 1895.

26. Louis Vauxcelles, "Claude Monet", in *L'Amour de l'Art*, August 1922, p. 231–235.

27. cf. R. Koechlin, "Claude Monet" in *Art et Décoration*, February 1927, p. 44.

28. Roger Fry, *Characteristics of French Art*, 1932, p. 127.

29. .cf. W. Weisbach, *Impressionismus – Ein Problem der Malerei in der Antike und Neuzeit*, Berlin, 1910–11, Vol. II, p. 141, quoted by John Rewald, *The History of Impressionism*, fourth revised edition, London, 1985, p. 564. Thames and Hudson.

30. J.J. Sweeney, *Plastic Redirections in 20th Century Painting*, Chicago, 1934, p. 6. also quoted by G.H. Hamilton, *op. cit.*

31. Lionello Venturi, *Impressionists and Symbolists*, Charles Scribner's Sons Ltd, New York, 1950, p. 65.

32. Eugene Boudin, letter, sale at Paris-Drouot, 25 June 1975, lot no. 176. Quoted in parts in Daniel Wildenstein, *op. cit.* Vol III, p. 66 and in *Hommage à Claude Monet*, 1980, p. 294.

33. cf. Janine Bailly-Herzberg, *Correspondance de Camille Pissarro*, Vol. IV, p. 69.

34. *Ibid.*, p. 71.

35. *Ibid.*, p. 74.

36. *Ibid.*, p. 75.

37. *Ibid.*, p. 78.

38. John Rewald, "Journal inédit de Paul Signac", *Gazette des Beaux-Arts*, July-Sept. 1949, also quoted in part in D. Wildenstein, *op. cit.*, Vol. III, p. 66.

39. John Rewald, *op. cit.*, p. 120; D.W., *op. cit.*, p. 66.

40. *Ibid.*

41. *cf.* J. B.-H., *op. cit.*, Vol. IV, p. 77.

42. *Ibid.*

43. We are here very grateful to Michel Hoog for his precious remarks on the posterity of Monet, published as the last chapter of *Hommage à Claude Monet*, Réunion des Musées Nationaux, Paris, 1980, p. 347–354, under the title "Note sur la postérité de Monet". In respect to Liebermann's reactions, he refers to M. Liebermann, "Monet – Anekdoten" in *Kunst und Künstler*, Vol. XXV, pp. 162–173.

44. *Ibid.*, p. 347.

45. K. Malevich, "Esthetics" in *Nova Gueneratsiya*, Kharkov, 1929, no. 12, p. 68. (translated from the French translation by V. & J.C. Marcadé) quoted by M. Hoog, *op. cit.*, p. 349.

46. *Ibid.*

47. K. Malevich, "Of the new art systems", Vitebsk, 1919, translated in Malevich, *De Cézanne au Suprématisme*, Lausanne, 1974, p. 103.

48. J.D Rey, *Plaisir de France*, Sept. 1971, p. 2, also quoted by Michel Hoog, *op. cit.*, p. 354.

49. Roy Liechtenstein in an interview by John Coplans, in John Coplans, *Roy Liechtenstein*, 1970.

50. Clement Greenberg, "Claude Monet, The later Monet", in *Art News*, Nov. 1956, Part II, p. 156.

EPILOGUE

1. *cf* George Heard Hamilton, "Cézanne and his critics", in *Cézanne, the Late Work*, edited by W. Rubin, 1977, p.139–149, The Museum of Modern Art, New York.

2. Liliane Brion-Guerry, "The Elusive Goal", in *Cézanne, the Late Work, op.cit.*, p.73–82.

3. D. Mirbeau, preface to *Claude Monet-Auguste Rodin*, Catalogue for an exhibition, quoted by John House, *Monet: Nature into Art*, 1986, p.221, Yale University Press, New Haven and London.

4. *cf* Stuckey, *Monet: A Retrospective, op.cit.*, p.165, Galley Press.

5. Wildenstein, *op.cit.*, Vol III, p.59–60.

6. *cf* George Heard Hamilton, "Cézanne, Bergson and the Image of Time", in *College Art Journal*, Fall 1956, Vol. XVI, no.1, p.2–12, New York

7. Auguste Comte, quoted by G.H. Hamilton, *op.cit.*, p.4

8. *Ibid.*, p.4–5.

9. *Ibid.*, p.5.

BIBLIOGRAPHICAL ADDENDA

Georges Clemenceau, "Revolution des Cathédrales", in *Grand Pan*, 1896, Paris, Fasquelle, p. 436. Referred to in the Introduction, p. 7, second last paragraph.

Janine Bailly-Herzberg, *Correspondance de Camille Pissarro*, Vol. IV, Paris, 1989, Editions du Valhermeil, p. 75 and 78. Referred to in the Introduction, p. 7, last paragraph.

D. Wildenstein, *Claude Monet: Biographie et Catalogue Raisonné*, Vol. III, p. 247. Referred to in the Origins chapter, p. 11, paragraph 6.

Janine Bailly-Herzberg, *Correspondance de Camille Pissarro*, Vol. I, Paris, 1980, Presses Universitaires de France, p. 241. Referred to in In Front of the Cathedral chapter, p. 15, paragraph 2.

H.Johsen and H. Bang, quoted in J. P. Hoschedé, *Claude Monet, ce mal connu*, Geneva, 1960, p. 110 and 112. Referred to in the Motif chapter, p. 21, paragraph 4.

Liliane Brion-Guerry, "The Elusive Goal", in *Cézanne, the late work*, New York, 1977, p. 82. Referred to in the Motif chapter, p. 23, second last paragraph.

Paul Valéry, quoted by Maurice Blanchot, *Le livre à venir*, Paris, 1953, p. 289. Referred to in the Motif chapter, p. 23, last paragraph.

Note: Throughout the footnotes Wildenstein refers to Daniel Wildenstein and JBH refers to Janine Bailly-Herzberg. Every effort has been made to check attributions and obtain permission from copyright holders. The editor apologizes for any errors or omissions which may have occurred.

THE PLATES

The sequence of plates which follows has been arranged according to each location. The successive times of day identified are approximate, based on analysis of the pictorial effects and of the evidence in Monet's letters.

All paintings dated by the artist carry the date 1894, indicating that they were signed and dated after reworkings at Monet's studio over a period of time following his second trip to Rouen in 1893.

PLATE 1
AFTERNOON
LOCATION: OUTDOORS, COUR D'ALBANE

This view of the cathedral and its counterpart (Plate 2), showing the Tour Saint Romain from the courtyard behind, are the only two close-up views executed outdoors. The layout and vantage point of the two compositions are similar, the houses attached to the tower are displayed almost identically. This painting, having a slightly wider format, includes a portion of the main wall of the cathedral.

Within an overall harmony of blues and purples, a strong cobalt blue line delineates the solid mass of the cathedral against the azure sky. There is a deeply human resonance to the image: the tall, imposing tower is plotted in the midst of a heap of houses milling with life, pierced with recesses and windows. These windows were painted by Monet in all sorts of colours – turquoise, green, lemon yellow, cerulean blue – thus formidably animating the whole surface of the painting and emphasizing, perhaps, their vital function as sources of light in life and of colour in painting.

La Cour d'Albane
92 × 73 cm (36 × 28¾ in)
Signed and dated at lower right
Smith College Museum of Art, Northampton, Mass.

PLATE 2
AFTERNOON
LOCATION: OUTDOORS, COUR D'ALBANE

In this painting the area of sky is considerably more worked out than in the previous image. It is cemented with grey-ochre paint, tinged with mauve, seeming to lose its colour on the stone of the tower. In this sombre yet vibrating harmony the windows, here too, are alive with light. They are painted in green, light blue-grey and dashes of yellow, setting a stark contrast with the ominous dark hole of the tunnel passing underneath the houses that leads to the other side of the cathedral, the west front.

The details in Monet's two views of the Tour Saint Romain are astonishing. In this painting, for instance, the combination of two sets of reflections depicted on the stone in grey/mauve and blue/grey with the light ochre and sienna undertones forms a particularly rich texture evoking the appearance of the tower in dull weather. Superimposed on this base are swarming touches of pink, crimson, yellow, green that tend to be absorbed in the underlying texture. There is evidence that Monet used a palette knife as well as a brush; for example, in the right vertical edge of the tower where the weight of the paint more pointedly marks the volume and density of the stone against the sky.

La Cour d'Albane (temps gris)
92 × 65 cm (36 × 25 ½ in)
Signed and dated at lower left
Private collection

PLATE 3
EARLY AFTERNOON (?)
LOCATION: LOUVET

Monet started two views of the cathedral (see also Plate 4) at the Louvet apartment, no. 31 Place de la Cathédrale, in February 1892 before interrupting work to spend time with his family at Giverny. The formats of these two initial views do not fit the standard format of the Louvet series. Possibly Monet started sketching the cathedral without a clear idea of how the image should evolve. These are the only views in the series to feature the neo-gothic spire that had been a nineteenth-century addition to the cathedral architecture.

It is difficult to assess the time of day, as the light is muted and rather sombre. The sky is made of a thick layer of grey-ochre, seemingly reflecting the colour of the earth. The clock is a grey paste encircled by a light slate-blue thread of paint with, at the centre, a touch of yellow ochre. The low-key harmony of the painting offers a neutral base as a starting point for the series. A comment by the poet Charles Péguy written about Monet's later *Waterlilies* series can also be applied with special relevance to this painting: "Since an illustrious painter has painted 27 or 35 times his famous waterlilies, when has he painted them best? Which one was best painted? The logical move would be to say: the last one, because the painter knew more. Well, I would say: on the contrary, the first one, because he knew less."

Le portail vue de face, harmonie brune
107 × 73 cm (42 × 28¾ in)
Signed and dated at lower left
Musée d'Orsay, Paris

PLATE 4
TIME OF DAY UNDEFINABLE
LOCATION: LOUVET

Although plate 3 shows signs of later reworking, this painting remained a simple oil sketch, perhaps indicating that Monet was unsatisfied with his first attempts. It has not been possible to reproduce this painting at full-page format.

Etude pour le portail vue de face
94 × 73 cm (37 × 28¾ in)
Signed but not dated, lower left
Private collection

PLATE 5
EARLY AFTERNOON: 1-2pm
LOCATION: LOUVET

Apart from the first two views, the paintings executed from the Louvet apartment offer a very strong cohesion, all executed on the same format and depicting effects of afternoon light. Since Monet worked at Louvet's in 1892 and 1893, some paintings in this group were initiated in each of those years. We know from Monet's letters that in 1892 he worked at the Louvet apartment in the late afternoon on what he called his "red and gold" motifs. Since this painting does not correspond to that description, and appears to show early afternoon light, it may be assumed that it was begun in 1893, when Monet was able to gain access to the apartment at different times of day.

The pale pink overtone of the painting relates it to Plates 10, 11 and 12, but it has greater nuances than the late afternoon views from the same location. The façade is brushed by a southern light, starting to move westward, gently shifting the shadows that fill the portal and rosace. The limited palette makes the image all the more effective. The brilliant blue of the sky is also applied to heightening the bones of the architecture, bringing the air itself right through the stone. An impression of gravity is reintroduced in the detail of the shadows, such as the bold trail of vermilion anchoring the right-hand edge of the central portal.

Le portail (soleil)
100 × 65 cm (39¼ × 25½ in)
Signed and dated at lower left
Private collection

PLATE 6
EARLY AFTERNOON: 2-3pm
LOCATION: LOUVET

As with the previous image, this painting is an early afternoon view likely to have been initiated in 1893. Two weeks before leaving Rouen in 1893, Monet wrote to his wife Alice that he was only then beginning to understand his subject. His letter included a startling description of the way the light was changing with the advance of the season: "Every day it is whiter; more and more it is blazing straight down...".

Here, in particular, the sunlight thoroughly drenches the stone façade. The contrasts are very subtle and subdued, with the hard edges of the architectural structure, heightened in green and gold paint, hardly sustained in three-dimensional terms. The blue shadows sprinkled on the façade recall a faded version of the sky, contributing to a yet more immaterial, ethereal impression. The paint surface is remarkably uneven. The crust of thick and richly blended colours in the shadows is offset by areas where the bare weave of the canvas remains visible. The painterly confidence of the image suggests that it may be one of the last works in the series. Everything is in motion, including the unusual detail of the three figures conspicuous in the foreground.

Le portail (soleil)
100 × 65 cm (39¼ × 25½ in)
Signed and dated at lower right
National Gallery of Art, Washington D.C.

PLATE 7
EARLY TO MID-AFTERNOON: 2.30–3.30pm
LOCATION: LOUVET

The light is gradually falling on the cathedral from the west, reducing the proportions of the shadows. The sun penetrates into the central portal, revealing the yellow-gold of the entrance door. Many structural details are emphatically delineated with blue brushstrokes offset against the light carnation pink of the overall surface. The contrast between sky and stone is more starkly portrayed than in the previous image. The sky is clearly composed of at least two layers of blue that give it a depth and solidity only enhanced by the warming mass of stone.

In the previous plate, the shadow colours seemed the logical chromatic continuation of the sunlit areas. Here the architecture is defined more intensely by green-golds and blues underlying the edges of the forms. Plate 6 demonstrates a progression of tones; plate 7 is based on aggressive contrasts.

Le portail (soleil)
100 × 65 cm (39¼ × 25½ in)
Signed and dated at lower left
Metropolitan Museum of Art, New York

PLATE 8
LATE AFTERNOON: 5-5.30pm
LOCATION: LOUVET

This painting is unmistakably the first of a group initiated at Louvet's in 1892. In a letter of 7 April 1892, Monet described the frustration of being unable to obtain access to the Louvet apartment, thereby being forced to interrupt his work on the "red and gold" motifs that he was painting there during the late afternoons. This painting begins a sequence that can be followed through in plates 9–12.

Whereas previously the cathedral was set in almost total isolation against the sky with a largely vertical emphasis, here the sun illuminates the western façade frontally, bleaching out the shadows on the stonework but introducing the creeping horizontal shadow thrown by the buildings standing opposite the cathedral. There is a confrontation of three main colour areas: the light purple base almost enclosing the strong orange and yellow shadows of the portals; the golden surface of the sun-drenched façade above; and the rich blue of the sky solidly visible between the cathedral towers. This triangular opposition is reinforced by the organization of the picture – the slightly oblique descending axis of the purple shadow from left to right offset by the oblique ascending axis of the crest of the façade, suggesting a triangular configuration whose third point extends somewhere beyond the left-hand side of the picture.

La Cathédrale de Rouen
100 × 65 cm (39¼ × 25½ in)
Signed and dated at lower left
Pushkin State Museum of Fine Arts, Moscow

PLATE 9

EARLY EVENING: 5.30-6pm
LOCATION: LOUVET

The line of cast shadow has risen to cover the central door but the top arch of the portal remains in the sun. The triangular configuration of shape and colour described in the previous commentary has become more obvious.

This painting, which retains the quality of an oil sketch rather than a completed, reworked image, provides some very interesting evidence as to Monet's working procedure. The paint is lightly worked over the whole surface except in the top of the cathedral portal – the meeting place of sun and shadow. Monet's priority was, therefore, to record what would no longer be visible a few moments later. Paradoxically, then, he caked up gold, vermilion and orange into a rising crust depicting the sun penetrating into the ribbed top of the portal. The sky has been composed of two layers – first a turquoise blue, then a colder tone, bringing the blue of the sky closer to the subdued hues of the shadows. Although this is clearly one of the evening works that Monet referred to as his "gold" motifs, the subtle pink reflecting the reddening sunset on the stone surface offers a perfect transition between the previous image (plate 8) and the following three paintings in this group.

Cathédrale de Rouen, effet de soleil, fin de journée
100 × 65 cm (39¼ × 25½ in)
Unsigned and undated, stamped with signature at lower right
Musée Marmottan, Paris

PLATE 10
LATE AFTERNOON: 5.30pm
LOCATION: LOUVET

The three red motifs follow each other in a clearly readable chronological sequence. The group is characterized by the increasingly blurred distinction between light and shadow. From the opposition of yellow-gold sunlight and purple shade in the previous two plates, the cathedral façade now carries a muffled opposition between the pink-red sunset hues and the growing purple-grey shadows. The shadow line has risen to the clock, placing a particular emphasis on this disc made of very light mauve paint, whose effect seems to radiate across the façade.

The signature on this painting is unusually far to the right and the painting remains undated. In the following two paintings the signature is painted in purplish-blue, in harmony with the rest of the picture, whereas here it is dark brown, suggesting that this was signed at a later date than the others.

Cathédrale de Rouen
100 × 65 cm (39¼ × 25½ in)
Signed at lower right, undated
Narodni Muzej, Belgrade

PLATE 11
EVENING: 6pm
LOCATION: LOUVET

The larger part of the façade is now in shadow. The shadow line has risen above the clock and reached nearly to the rosace. The effect of this painting evokes not only the last darting beams of the red sun, it also carries through the warmth of the stone after a whole afternoon of exposure to the sunlight. Interestingly, the shadow is partly made of warm tones of yellow and light, diluted oranges. Even the clock, a grey-mauve circle, has been given a yellow centre, emphasising the contrast of warmth and coldness as well as light and shade.

La Cathédrale de Rouen
100 × 65 cm (39¼ × 25½ in)
Signed and dated at lower left
Collection Larock-Granoff, Paris

57

PLATE 12
EVENING:6.30pm
LOCATION: LOUVET

This view appears chronologically the latest of the late afternoon and evening effects in the whole *Cathedral* series. The sunlight has now become too weak to impress a clear dividing line between sun and shadow. The purplish shadow clings to every nook of the façade, on the sides of the towers, in every crevice or interval.

The deep blue tones in the shadow are used to heighten certain details and underscore particular shapes that in a few moments will no longer be visible. Monet worked as late as he could, as long as the daylight lasted. In this painting we see the artist struggling not with the daylight – nor with the weather – but against the oncoming twilight. This painting sets a temporal limit to the series.

Cathédrale de Rouen, symphonie en gris et rose
100 × 65 cm (39¼ × 25½ in)
Signed and dated at lower left
National Museum of Wales, Cardiff

PLATE 13
TIME OF DAY UNDEFINABLE
LOCATION: LOUVET

Monet frequently complained in his letters about the bad weather in Rouen, grey weather effects are far fewer in the series than sunlit images. The two initial views from the Louvet apartment show a predominant greyness (plates 3 and 4), as does one view from the 1893 location at Mauquit's shop (plate 30). Monet's letters describe the initiation of "two or three grey weathers" in 1892. On 24 February 1893 he reported that he was, reluctantly, working once again on these effects because of the "continuing grey, grimy and slightly misty weather".

Despite the low-key atmosphere, the cathedral façade seems to ripple with architectural and sculptural detail, although lacking the strong chromatic oppositions that elsewhere describe the contrasts of light and shade. Vibrations in the stone are created through very subtle colour devices – a light pink undertone, silvery highlights, a richly intricate combination of sapphire blue, raw sienna, pink and purple displayed throughout the rosace and discreetly echoed in the clock. The sky, though at first sight monochromatic, is not grey but a gentle white tarnished with yellow and blue.

Le portail (temps gris)
100 × 65 cm (39¼ × 25½ in)
Signed and dated at lower left
Musée d'Orsay, Paris

PLATE 14
EARLY MORNING: 7-8am
LOCATION: LÉVY

The paintings initiated at Lévy's in 1892 were all morning and early afternoon effects, following Monet's schedule of working there until about 3pm, then moving to the Louvet apartment to work on his late afternoon effects. This appears to be one of the earliest morning views of the cathedral. The light is rising, gently touching the tips of the two small towers. At the level of the clock a few details become distinguishable – a spiral of light blue paint touched with pink and yellow suggests a cycle of light and dark, sun and shade, that has no beginning and no end. The mist still enveloping the lower half of the cathedral retains some nocturnal traces. The three portals can hardly be seen, wrapped and disguised by the invisible *enveloppe*. What technically distinguishes this painting from the others is an extraordinary unity in the brushwork, which follows a web of swift oblique and slightly curved strokes all over the canvas. The mist, the sky and the stone are bound together within this web of paint.

This painting was exhibited in the 1895 show at Durand-Ruel's as number one in the catalogue.

Le portail, brouillard matinal
100 × 65 cm (39¼ × 25½ in)
Signed and dated at lower left
Folkwang Museum, Essen

PLATE 15
MORNING: 8-9am
LOCATION: LÉVY

This painting seems to follow in sequence from the early morning view. The light of the "rosy-fingered dawn" warms the edges of the towers and blends gradually with the dissipating layers of morning mist, endowing them with a purple tinge. As the mist disappears it discreetly uncovers the orange doors of the portals. There is a suggestion of two figures standing in front of the portal to the left. As with plates 6 and 13 where figures are also visible, this counteracts the theory that the *Cathedral* paintings are "dehumanized".

The sky – an early morning sky – is composed of several layers of creamy colouring that hold a direct chromatic relation to the scheme of the cathedral façade.

Le portail (effet du matin)
100 × 65 cm (39¼ × 25½ in)
Signed and dated at lower left
Private collection

PLATE 16
MORNING: 8-9am
LOCATION: LÉVY

What is remarkable in several works in the Lévy group of paintings is that Monet seems to have conceived them in pairs. Plates 15 and 16 provide the first example. While the sunlight effect coming from the east is almost identical in both works, the prevailing chromatic harmony follows the same equation, but inverted between one painting and the next. In plate 15 the dominant hues are purple with pink undertones. In this painting, the effect is in reverse, the pink overlaid on purple undertones. The early sunlight seems to have gradually infiltrated the stone surface from behind, so that details such as the rosace become more readily discernible. The peak of the façade, standing directly against the light, retains more of the deep purple tone. Equally, definition between the base of the cathedral and the threshold remains unclear.

Le portail, effet de matin
100 × 65 cm (39¼ × 25½ in)
Signed and dated at lower left
Private collection

PLATE 17
MORNING: 9-10am
LOCATION: LÉVY

After the cathedral has shed the purples and pinks of the rising sun gradually illuminating the stone, a completely different tonality takes over. The light, indicated with patches of clear yellow, turns the edges and crests of the façade into silvery grey. The warm light bathing the top of the cathedral is in gentle confrontation with the remaining shadow, described with cold, pale blues offset with a myriad small strokes of green subtly infused into the crust of paint. The sky, like all the morning skies in the Lévy series, is composed of muted tones – white, light blues and yellows unmixed but forming a subdued green base. Even the clock seems to confirm this singular chromatic composition: it is composed of a swirling, broken spiral of blue on a pale yellow circle.

Le portail
100 × 65 cm (39¼ × 25½ in)
Signed and dated at lower left
Kunstsammlungen zu Weimar, Schlossmuseum, Weimar

PLATE 18
MORNING: 9-10am
LOCATION: LÉVY

This painting can be seen to form a pair with the previous image. The sunlight is shed on the cathedral from the south-east, halfway to the noon effect when the shadow line becomes exactly parallel to the western façade. The central pinnacle of the cathedral is half-lit, although the base of the triangle remains in shade. The difference between the two paintings therefore lies more in the study of the weather effects, or the *enveloppes*, than of the time of day.

The light is more evenly spread, the details of the portal more visible. The skies are very close in tone and colour in these two paintings, but in this version the sky has a thickness and consistency comparable to the paint surface describing the cathedral. The prevailing harmony of hues is more complex. The yellow light seems to have lost its brightness in the density of the atmosphere. The contrast of light and shade on the façade relies on blues and purples.

Le portail
100 × 65 cm (39¼ × 25½ in)
Signed and dated at lower left
National Gallery of Art, Washington D.C.

PLATE 19
LATE MORNING: 11.45am-12 noon
LOCATION: LÉVY

This painting and the canvas shown in plate 20 were executed in different formats from that standard for paintings of the Louvet and Lévy groups in the series. This indicates that Monet was interested in experimenting with the format as one of his compositional devices. The proportions are less elongated, more compact, offering less space for the square in front of the cathedral that usually occupies a part of the foreground and also cutting through the central pinnacle and truncating the towers. In general terms, the sky and the earth are less visible in this format.

The tumbled texture of the sky indicates changeable weather. This impression is emphasized by the alternating warm and cold hues and areas at the peak of the façade and left tower that appear darkened by shadow, while the base of the cathedral reflects the golden sunlight. In his letters Monet frequently complained of the "ceaseless changes" of weather and recorded particularly rapid and dramatic shifts of atmosphere – from rain to snow to sunshine – in mid-March 1893, when he was reworking some of the Lévy paintings.

Le portail, harmonie bleue
91 × 63 cm (35¾ × 24¾ in)
Signed and dated at lower right
Musée d'Orsay, Paris

PLATE 20
NOON
LOCATION: LÉVY

In the balance of colours and overall layout, this painting seems very close in time to the previous version. There, the shadow zone in front of the cathedral appears slightly thicker and more pronounced in the portals, indicating the slightly earlier time. Here, the line of shadow is perfectly parallel to the façade: the light is coming from due south. The thin blue shadow hugs the walls and the ground in front of the cathedral is in full light.

The colour contrasts in this painting are more intense. The pinks turn to golds, the oranges are sharpened. The definition of the left tower against the sky is more clearly asserted, with no cloud darkening its form. The pinnacle of the façade seems to retain some of the colour of the sky, as it is delineated with strong blue lines. It also takes the cast shadow of the Tour de Buerre, to the right of the portal but not seen in this painting. The clock stands out in the light, a circle of pink surrounded by golden yellow and touched with blue and red.

Cathédrale de Rouen, portail plein midi
106 × 73 cm (41 1/2 × 28 3/4 in)
Signed and dated at lower right
Sterling and Francine Clark Institute, Williamstown, Mass.

PLATE 21
MIDDAY: 12.30-1pm
LOCATION: LÉVY

Monet clearly felt a particular interest in the effects of midday light on the cathedral. In a letter to Alice Hoschedé on 5 April 1892, he explained that he would take an early break for lunch on sunny days, around 11am, as it was essential to be at work from 12 noon to 2pm.

This painting exhibits a clear, brilliantly blue sky, in contrast to previous paintings in the Lévy series. The sky is painted in cobalt blue heightened with white. The same blue is used throughout the shadows on the façade, though these are also shot through with tinges of purple. The purple strokes are offset by the golden yellow and orange tones, directly balancing the cold effects of the blue-purple shadows. The third element in the chromatic arrangement of this image is the creamy near-white that confers the structural definition of the cathedral. The pale detail of the stone under midday sunlight is warmed by pink and gold undertones.

Cathédrale de Rouen, effet de soleil
100 × 65 cm (39¼ × 25½ in)
Signed and dated at lower left
Museum of Fine Arts, Boston

PLATE 22
MIDDAY TO EARLY AFTERNOON: 1-2pm
LOCATION: LÉVY

The nearly perfect balance between light and shadow has started to tip over. The pinnacle of the cathedral is now almost completely illuminated by a south-south-west light. Likewise the turret in the top right corner of the picture gradually receives a warming light during this period when the sun is at its hottest. The shadow line has begun to recede obliquely inside the portals. The light begins to penetrate, wrapping around more details on the stone surface, underscoring the protrusions and throwing it into sharper relief. The light is gently gilding the stone and the areas of orange and gold have increased proportionately against the indigo shadows of the previous view. In this painting the intensity of the blues is fading, giving way to pale Naples yellow striking up the lit edges of the stone.

Le portail
92 × 65 cm (36 × 25 ½ in)
Signed at lower left, undated
Private collection

PLATE 23
EARLY TO MID-AFTERNOON: 2-3pm
LOCATION: LÉVY

The final pair of paintings in the Lévy series of 1892, plates 23 and 24, are the afternoon effects that Monet worked on each day just before moving to his other location, the Louvet apartment, to continue work on the late afternoon paintings. While these two are the latest of the afternoon paintings from Lévy's, they also compare with one of the views from Louvet's probably begun in 1893, plate 6. This shows a similar time of day but the season is different. Whereas this pair relates to work during February of 1892, plate 6 is illuminated by the late spring light of April, more vertical than oblique, whitening and all-pervasive.

The wintry light of this painting seems to support the cathedral with a scaffolding of pale blue shadow lines, which heighten the structural details of the façade, whereas the stronger spring light of plate 6 seems to scorch the surface and eat up the detail, even the shadow. The higher degree of "realism" in the Cathedral paintings is achieved when the greater balance between light and shadow exists, as here and in plate 24.

Le portail et la Tour Saint Romain, plein soleil
107 × 73 cm (42 × 28¾ in)
Signed and dated at lower left
Musée d'Orsay, Paris

PLATE 24

EARLY TO MID-AFTERNOON: 2-3pm
LOCATION: LÉVY

See previous commentary. It has not been possible to reproduce this painting at full page format.

Cathédrale de Rouen
106 × 73 cm (41 1/2 × 28 3/4 in)
Signed and dated at lower left
Private collection

PLATE 25

MORNING
LOCATION: MAUQUIT

The vantage point at Monet's new location in 1893, the shop belonging to M. Mauquit, was very similar to the view he had taken from Lévy's boutique in the year before, therefore Monet was able to rework some of the Lévy paintings as well as initiate new effects. This partly explains why only six new paintings are identifiable from 1893, since much of Monet's time was absorbed by reworkings.

A characteristic of the Mauquit series is that Monet apparently felt able to take more liberties with his subject, becoming more innovative and audacious. His interest in effects of mist and fog was well known, and was a particular feature of his London paintings. In fact, he claimed that it was the fog that made London into a beautiful city: "Its regular, massive blocks become grandiose in this mysterious cloak." This painting of the cathedral in mist is an extreme case of what is at stake throughout the *Cathedral* series. One could say, ironically, that the fog sharpens Monet's creative process. The universe is undermined by the undefinable, the visible reality altered by the invisible. The witness of this transformation cannot restore its ideal stability. Monet recurrently described his work at Rouen as "a search for the impossible".

Le cathédrale dans le brouillard
106 × 73 cm (41 1/2 × 28 3/4 in)
Signed and dated at lower left
Private collection

PLATE 26
EARLY MORNING: 8-8.30am
LOCATION: MAUQUIT

This and the following two plates offer interesting examples of Monet's pictorial experiments from the Mauquit location in 1893. All depict approximately the same time of day, between 8 and 9 in the morning with the sunlight rising and exposing the back of the Tour Saint Romain. This tower, previously partly cut off by the picture frame, is now fully included within the image, with its neighbouring houses. The small turret to the right of the pinnacle and Tour de Beurre, usually placed at the extreme right have gone.

The base of the cathedral lightens perceptibly through the three images: the features of the houses at the side become progressively more defined. However, this indicates not so much a chronological sequence as Monet's concern with composing pictorial variations on the same theme – the Tour Saint Romain against the light of dawn. The surface of this painting is remarkable in its solid thickness. One senses that it has been worked as layer over layer of heavy paint. The colour contrasts are strong, evoking the dawn light bursting through the density of night.

Le portail et la Tour Saint Romain a l'Aube
106 × 74 cm (41¾ × 29 in)
Signed and dated at lower left
Museum of Fine Arts, Boston

PLATE 27
MORNING: 8.30-9am
LOCATION: MAUQUIT

The contrast is most intense here between the radiating lemon yellow of the sunrise and the dark blue shadow still staining the larger portion of the façade. This is perhaps the painting that most vividly depicts the ascending and transient movement of the sunlight in relation to the earth. Everything in the composition seems to corroborate this momentary spectacle. In the narrow vertical band of sky at the left, the light passes from deep yellow to a barely defined blue-green. The tower, dissolving into sunlight above its nocturnal base, displays a crescendo of hues – from deep ultramarine to an almost diaphanous yellow – that is complementary and opposed to the order of colours in the sky. To the right of the composition, the three central elements of the cathedral – the pointed arch of the central portal, the triangular spire containing the clock and above that the pinnacle of the façade – seem to systematize the movement of light in the painting by pointing conspicuously upward.

This is the largest painting of the entire series. A feature of the Mauquit group of paintings is that they were painted on larger size canvases of irregular format.

Le portail (effet du matin)
110 × 73 cm (43 ¼ × 28 ¾ in)
Signed and dated at lower left
Ernst Beyeler Collection

PLATE 28
MORNING: 8.15-9.15am
LOCATION: MAUQUIT

The cathedral seems here to undergo an effect of harmonization. The stark contrasts of the previous two images are gone. The light reverberates on the façade, giving sharper definition to the details, such as the distinct components of the left and central portals and the small columns just above the rosace. The chromatic description of light and dark is a gradation rather than an opposition of tones. Yellow-pink light gently suffuses the façade through the intertices and merges into a cooler, deeper purplish tone at the right. The flight of crows scattering around the tower brings in an anecdotal element that provoked some comment in the press reviews of the 1895 Durand-Ruel exhibition.

Le portail et la Tour Saint Romain (effet du matin)
106 × 73 cm (41¾ × 28¾ in)
Signed and dated at lower left
Musée d'Orsay, Paris

PLATE 29
NOON
LOCATION: MAUQUIT

This painting forms a transition between the Lévy series (plates 14 to 24) and the Mauquit group (plates 25 to 30). A thin, vertical portion of the houses attached to the Tour Saint Romain is visible at the left. In the remaining paintings of the Mauquit group the houses become more visible, although the arrangement of the composition on the right-hand side of the canvas is similar in all the paintings. The variation in this painting is attributable to the slightly narrower format of the canvas.

In other respects, however, this painting does not seem quite to fit in with its companions. It more closely relates to plates 6 and 7, which appear to be among the last that Monet started. It suggests the same effect of the white, blazing sunlight of late spring described by Monet. Interestingly, it also matches the format of the other two "white" paintings.

Le portail
100 × 65 cm (39¼ × 25½ in)
Signed and dated at lower left
Pushkin State Museum of Fine Arts, Moscow

PLATE 30
TIME OF DAY UNDEFINABLE
LOCATION: MAUQUIT

This painting presents an interesting paradox. While the *enveloppe* of grey weather, heavy with rain, is dim, grimy and woolly, the cathedral façade is presented with more detail of the architecture and sculpture than in the majority of the series paintings: one can almost discern the sculptured figures that border the clock spire

The harmony and unity of colours are also rarely observed elsewhere in the series. Stark oppositions or contrasts are scarcely to be found in this painting. It is organized around a harmonious rhythm of sombre blues, greys and siennas, with a very light pink as undertone. The only exception to this is the tiny dot of orange at the centre of the clock, perhaps pointing out that the sun is not so far behind this pall of grey weather.

Le portail et la Tour Saint Romain, temps gris
100 × 73 cm (39¼ × 28¾ in)
Signed and dated at lower left
Musée des Beaux-Arts, Rouen

THE CATHEDRAL SERIES

The number accompanying each plate in this sequence refers to the number assigned to each painting in Daniel Wildenstein's *Monet: Biographie et Catalogue Raisonné.*

Plate 1   W. 1317

Plate 2   W. 1318

Plate 5   W. 1322

Plate 6   W. 1324

Plate 3   W. 1319

Plate 4   W. 1320

Plate 7   W. 1325

Plate 8   W. 1326

Plate 9   W. 1327

Plate 10   W. 1329

Plate 11   W. 1328

Plate 12   W. 1323

Plate 13   W. 1321

Plate 14   W. 1352

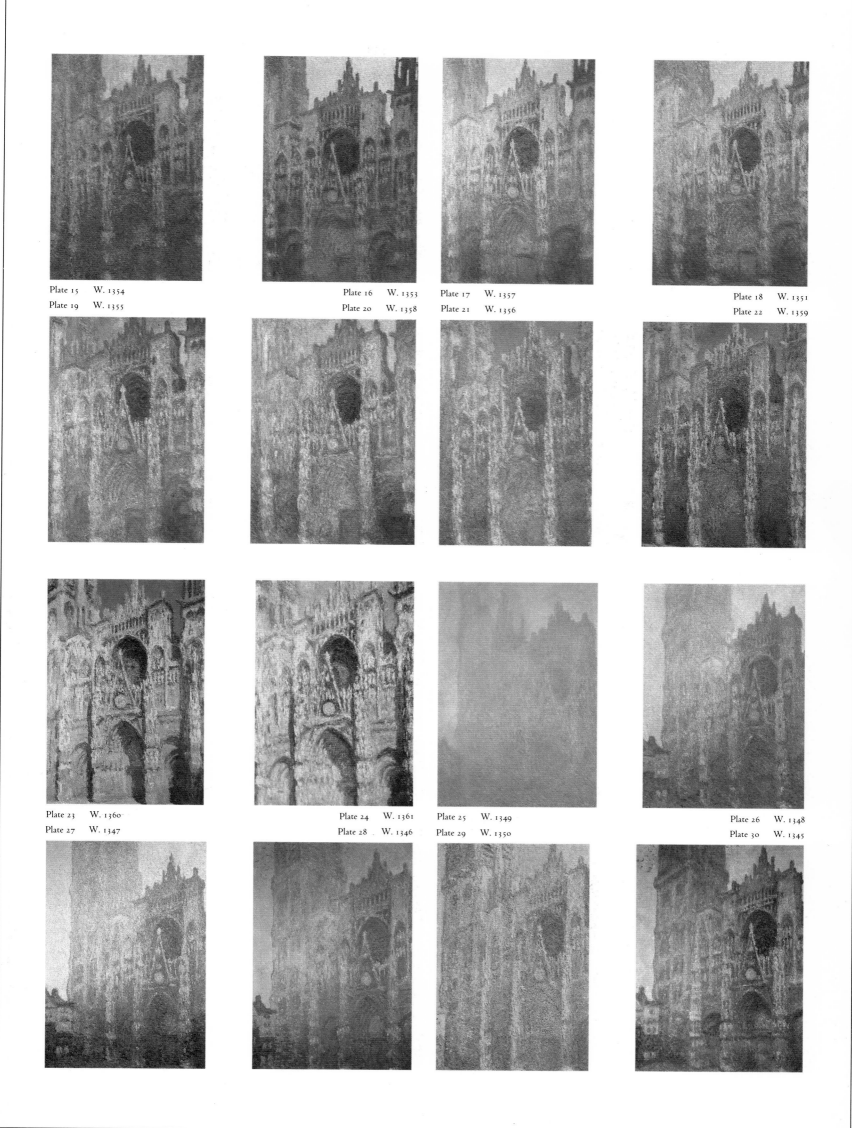

Plate 15   W. 1354
Plate 19   W. 1355

Plate 16   W. 1353
Plate 20   W. 1358

Plate 17   W. 1357
Plate 21   W. 1356

Plate 18   W. 1351
Plate 22   W. 1359

Plate 23   W. 1360
Plate 27   W. 1347

Plate 24   W. 1361
Plate 28   W. 1346

Plate 25   W. 1349
Plate 29   W. 1350

Plate 26   W. 1348
Plate 30   W. 1345

ACKNOWLEDGEMENTS

From the inception of this project, onwards, I have received much support and encouragement from individuals and institutions to whom I am deeply grateful.

I am particularly indebted to private collectors, most of whom prefer to remain anonymous, for having been so generous in providing photographic or archival material. I wish to thank namely Ernst Beyeler, Pierre Larock, and Masahiko Sawada. I would also like to stress my gratitude to the staffs of all the following institutions and in particular: in France, at the Musée d'Orsay: Françoise Cachin, Sylvie Patin, and Anne Distel; at the Centre de Documentation du Musée d'Orsay: Anne Roquebert; and at the Bibliothèque of the Musée d'Orsay: Bernadette Buiret and Marie-France Bougie; at the Musée du Louvre, (Département de Conservation): Charles de Couessin; at the Musée Marmottan, Paris: Arnaud d'Hauterives, Caroline Genet; at the Musée des Beaux-Arts et de la Céramique, of Rouen, François Bergot and Gilles Grandjean; the staff of the Bibliothèque Municipale and Cabinet des Estampes de Rouen; the staff of the Bibliothèque d'Art et d'Archéologie (Fondation Jacques Doucet), and the staff of the Bibliothèque Nationale, Paris. In Germany, at the Kunstsammlungen zu Weimar (Schlossmuseum): Rainer Krauss; at the Museum Folkwang (Museen der Stadt, Essen): Dr Georg W. Költzsch. In Japan, at the Bridgestone Museum: Tatsuji Ohmori, Curator; at the National Museum of Western Art, Tokyo: Koji Yukiyama. In the U.S.A., at the Museum of Fine Arts, Boston: Alan Shestack, Barbara Shapiro; at the Sterling and Francine Clark Art Institute, Williamstown: David S. Brooke; at the Metropolitan Museum of Art, New York: Gary Tinterow, Katharine Baetjer and Carmel Wilson; at the National Gallery of Art, Washington, D.C.: Charles Moffett, Nan Rosenthal; at the Smith College Museum of Art, Northampton: Edward Nygren, Michael Goodison; at the Toledo Museum of Art: Lee Mooney. In the U.S.S.R., at the Pushkin State Museum of Fine Arts, Inna Orn, Nina Kalitina, Anna Barskaya, and Eugenia Georgievskaya. In the U.K., at the National Gallery: Neil McGregor, John Leighton; at the British Museum: Paul Dove; at the Royal Academy: Norman Rosenthal and Mary Anne Stevens; at the Victoria and Albert Museum: Edwin Wallace; at the National Museum of Wales: Rosalind Freeman and Tim Egan; the staff of the Courtauld Library, and the Staff of the National Gallery's library, especially Elspeth Hector. In Yugoslavia, at the Narodni Muzej, Belgrad: Jetva Jevtovic, Nikola Kusovac and Irina Subotic.

My thanks go to Caroline Godfroy Durand-Ruel and France Daguet at the Archives Durand-Ruel, whose help in the research for this book has been essential. The Fondation Wildenstein has provided, under the guidance of Daniel Wildenstein, ceaseless help, suggestions and material; I wish to thank in particular Rodolphe Walter and Thérèse Nanus in Paris; and Ay-Whang Hsia in New York.

I am indebted to the following individuals who have contributed invaluably to making this book possible: Nicolas Beurret; His Excellency the Japanese Ambassador in London, Kazuo Chiba; at Christie's, London: James Roundell and Lady Selina Chenevière; at Christie's New York: Michael Findlay, Frank Giraud and Diana Kunkel; at Citibank, New York: Kevin Buchanan and Christine De Metruis; Jeffrey Deitch; Ellen and Paul Josefowitz; at the Lefevre Gallery: Desmond Corcoran and Martin Summers; Daniel Malingue; Marzina Marzetti; Mary Jo McLoughlin; Toshihisa Ono, cultural attache, Embassy of Japan; Manuel Schmit; at Sotheby's London: Michel Strauss and Marjorie Delpech; at Sotheby's New York: David Nash, Judy Murphy and Diana Hamilton-Jones; Guy Weill-Goudchaux; Lady Jacqueline Weir; John Whately, and Sabine Yi.

I also wish to mention those scholars who either through their work or conversation have offered great insight, in particular: Hélène Adhemar; Janine Bailly-Herzberg; Richard Brettell; Liliane Brion-Guerry; Douglas Druick; Georges Duby; Luc Ferry; John Gage; Robert Gordon; George Heard Hamilton; Michael Hoog; John House; Clare Joyes; Michael Kauffmann; Richard Kendall; Christopher Lloyd; Jean-Luc Marion; Michel Melot; Alain Renaut; John Rewald; Grace Seiberling; Charles Stuckey; Paul Hayes Tucker (who also very kindly helped secure important transparencies); Roland Vasseur. My greatest debt is to Daniel Wildenstein, whose meticulous analysis of Monet's oeuvre is a cornerstone to any study of Monet today.

I am also most thankful to Fiona Barclay, Veronique Bourgarel, Paula Breslich, Raymonde Carpentier, Gregory French, Natasha Livit, Judy Martin, Alan Osband, Katia Pissarro, Cathy Stubbs and Laura Wilson for their various and much appreciated contributions, to Eric Shanes for having initiated the idea of this book, to Louise Scalia for her tireless and methodical work on this manuscript and to Annabel for her invaluable contributions to this book.

PHOTOGRAPHY CREDITS
Illustration on page 13 (top right): Studio Patrick Goetelen
Illustrations on page 15: Studio Lourmel 77, Paris
Plates 2, 9, 22: Studio Lourmel 77, Paris
Plate 17: Roland Dressler, Weimar
Plates 19, 23, 28: Lauros-Giraudon, Paris
Plate 30: Photo Ellebé, Rouen